THE
BEGATITUDES

WHAT'S IN A NAME

ADAM • CAIN • ABEL • SETH

ENOSH • CAINAN • MAHALALEL

JARED • ENOCH • METHUSELAH

LAMECH • NOAH

HOWARD GREEN

DEDICATION

This book is dedicated first and foremost to the Lord Jesus. It is His great name that I want to glorify through the names of the biblical patriarchs in these pages. Without Christ my life would be dull and uneventful. With Christ there is rarely a dull moment. I choose the excitement of being in His service, although I appreciate the down times too. May God receive the praise for any blessing received from reading this book.

Second, I want to thank my parents, Ray and Betty Green, for early on causing me to have a "drug" problem. They drug me to Sunday School, they drug me to church services, they drug me to Vacation Bible School, and they drug me to revival services. And when we weren't at church, they drug me to the television set and made me watch Billy Graham crusades! God bless them.

I also want to thank my wonderful family. My wife and children have been a special blessing to me. They have faithfully supported and encouraged me in the writing of this book. In fact, they were supportive long before it was even a dream. They have stood with me in the brilliant decisions I have made and in the not-so-brilliant ones. Thank you, Debbie, wife of patience and faith, and thank you, Amy and Tommy, children with selective memories.

◆

CONTENTS

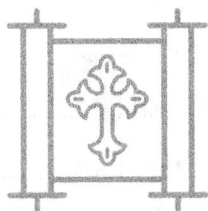

INTRODUCTION

The God of all creation has always planned to have a people on whom He could lavish His amazing love. His original intention was for it to happen in the garden of Eden. When Adam foiled that plan, the Father was not deterred. He already knew what He was going to do. That is why Jesus is referred to as the "Lamb slain from the foundation of the world" (Revelation 13:8). The apostle Peter says of the Messiah, "He indeed was foreordained before the foundation of the world, but was manifest in these last times for you" (1 Peter 1:20).

In Genesis 5:3–32 we read the names of the first ten patriarchs, from Adam to Noah. In the meanings of these names God reveals His story for the redemption of humanity. A study of these names also reveals how God will go about implementing His plan through Christ. In other words, each name reveals an aspect of Christ's saving of humanity. Our God is truly one who does all things decently and in order. The meaning of each name uncovers a part of the Father's plan of salvation, including the humanity of Jesus, His resurrection, and His bringing us into the peace that God provides.

The title *Begatitude* is a play on words. Jesus's inspiring Sermon on the Mount (Matthew 5–7) begins with what we refer to as the Beatitudes (Matthew 5:3–12). For some of us the meaning is that Jesus is speaking these words to us as *beautiful attitudes.* Along the same line of thought, the word *Begatitude* is being used to speak of a "begotten-to-reveal-Christ attitude." The word is meant to emphasize the fact that these patriarchs were begotten, or born, and given their individual names for the purpose of pointing to the life and saving grace of Jesus.

The Old Testament is given to us to direct our attention to the Christ and His God-given mission to redeem humanity. The feasts, the sacrifices, and the laws foreshadowed Jesus and were fulfilled in Jesus (Matthew 5:17). In like manner these ten names are God's subtle revelation of the salvation He offers to humanity in His Son, Jesus the Messiah.

All that God has done throughout history, or better yet, *His story,* has been for the redemption of humanity. His remarkable plan of revealing this begins as He gives names that will be shadows or types of the coming Christ. Let there be no mistake: God is all about rescuing the perishing. His passion is to save the lost. And the very first book of the Holy Bible and the very first created and begotten humans testify to this great truth.

As you dig more deeply into the meanings of these names on your own, you will likely find a wealth of truth that has not been included in these chapters. So "be diligent to present yourself approved to God, a worker who does not need to be ashamed, rightly dividing the word of truth" (2 Timothy 2:15).

Included in the ten names of the men who are direct ancestors of Christ are the names of *Cain* and *Abel,* found in chapters two and three. These two names are not seen in Genesis 5:3–32 because both men were disqualified from being in the Savior's lineage. Abel was murdered, Cain was banished, but the meanings of their names still carry a prophecy of what was to happen in the life of Christ. For this reason their names will be a part of this study. So we will actually be processing the meanings of twelve names.

It is also interesting to note that the word *name* is *shem* in Hebrew and can mean "reputation," "fame," "glory," "memorial," or "monument." Each of these men was called by a name that was to be his fame or glory. Each had a position, a place, in telling the salvation story. Of all the names these men could have been called by, isn't it astonishing that each of them was given a name that revealed an aspect of the Savior's life? Our God is very clever in the subtlety of telling us something without putting it on a silver platter. In the case of the first patriarchs, He was revealing how He was going to save humanity from His own wrath.

Solomon tells us in Proverbs 25:2, "It is the glory of God to conceal a matter, but the glory of kings is to search out a matter." This verse is a clue to us that the truths we find in the Word of God are not always on the surface of what we are reading. To find the pure gold we sometimes have to use a pick and shovel. In other words, if the gold is worth finding, it is worth digging for. The gold in God's Word is worth finding.

Another aspect of this study is to bring to our attention the fact that we really don't know very much about the lives of these twelve men. We know Adam's claim to fame and Cain's dastardly deed. We know that Abel died young. But what do we really know about Enosh or Cainan or Mahalalel or Jared? We know more about Noah than any of them, and he is the last of the twelve in this study. The truth is that most of what can be known about them is in the meanings of their names. And their names are important only because each reveals an attribute of our Savior.

And that is the primary purpose of the names of these patriarchs. God used them to help us understand His primary and passionate purpose. That purpose, of course, was and is to save humanity. God will have a people for himself. From Adam to Noah, God reveals to us that plan. He does it without telling us much about their lives, but a wealth of revelation can be seen in their names.

There is another piece to this puzzle that is as wondrous as the meanings found in the names of these twelve men. It is the number *twelve* itself. It is the fourth of the four perfect numbers found in the Holy Bible. The other three are *three, seven,* and *ten.* (There are several good books written on the subject of numerology that will give you a detailed description of the four perfect numbers.

Two of these books are *Number in Scripture: Its Supernatural Design and Spiritual Significance,* by E. W. Bullinger, and *Biblical Mathematics: Keys to Scripture Numerics,* by Ed F. Vallowe.) Each of those four numbers represents a perfect condition of the kingdom of God. For this study only the number *twelve* is relevant.

Twelve represents perfect government. There were the twelve sons of Jacob, whose name was changed to Israel. He went from being a deceiver to being a prince of God. Talk about moving on up! Israel's twelve sons are the governing bodies in the Old Testament, the twelve tribes of Israel. In the New Testament it is the twelve apostles who govern (Matthew 10:2–4). Jesus was twelve years old when He told His parents that He must be about His Father's business (Luke 2:42). When Jesus fed the five thousand, the apostles took up twelve baskets of leftovers, each representing one of the apostles chosen to govern. The woman with the issue of blood had been afflicted for twelve years (Matthew 9:20). The daughter of Jairus whom Jesus healed was twelve years old (Mark 5:42). Jesus said He could call twelve legions of angels to fight for Him (Matthew 26:53). In the book of the Revelation (21:12) we find twelve gates into the holy city, twelve angels at those gates, and the names of the twelve sons of Jacob written on the gates.

Each of the illustrations above speaks of God's perfect government. Isaiah prophesies of the Messiah's reign when he says, "Unto us a Child is born, unto us a Son is given; And the government will be upon His shoulder. And His name will be called Wonderful, Counselor, Mighty God, Everlasting Father, Prince of Peace. Of the increase of His government and peace there will be no end" (Isaiah 9:6–7).

Jesus rules over sickness and disease. He rules over all our needs. He rules over the holy city. It's interesting that God used the names of twelve men to signify His rule over salvation. "Nor is there salvation in any other, for there is no other name under heaven given among men by which we must be saved" (Acts 4:12)—*Yeshua*, King of kings and Lord of lords. What a mighty God we serve! He is wise and wonderful.

So what's in a name? In the twelve names of this study it is the revelation of the greatest gift ever offered to humanity! May you be blessed and inspired as you experience the removal of the veil that shrouds the names of God's first twelve signposts.

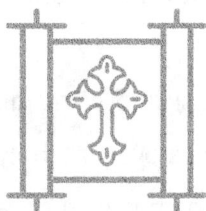

1

ADAM:
Man of Earth

God's plan to have a people to love begins with a man named *Adam,* pronounced "Aw-dawm." It means "red" and signifies that his body was created from the earth, or the red clay.

Adam was God's pride and joy. He was to be the first of a human family that would enjoy the benefits of the Father's love and blessings. Perhaps Yahweh sang over him as Adam was being formed, "This little light of Mine —I'm gonna make him shine!" Perhaps not. But maybe a little imagination is a good thing when attempting to see behind the curtain of the creation of our famous first father.

At any rate, Adam was created in the likeness and image of his Father. Adam was designed for greatness. He was to rule and reign over all of God's creation. He was given dominion over all the creatures in the garden. Adam was to love and care for the animals as the Father loved and cared for him, the first human being.

As a human being, Adam was both a physical being and a spiritual being. His body was a house in which his spirit and soul were to dwell. His body was of the natural, the earth; his spirit and soul were of the supernatural, the breath or life of God. He was indeed a wondrous and special being.

Not only was Adam created to reflect the image and likeness of the Creator, but he was also raised up to receive and deliver the unconditional love God had for him. He was to multiply and fill the earth with beings just like himself. Imagine a world where every human being thinks like God, acts like God, speaks like God. What a wonderful world that would be! And that day is soon coming, the day when every born-again human will know just how wonderful it is to live in a God-reflecting climate and atmosphere.

The similarities between the first Adam and the last Adam are likely already clear. We know that Jesus was God's pride and joy. In the very first chapter of the book of Hebrews God says of Christ, "'You are My Son, today I have begotten You.' And again: 'I will be to Him a Father, and He shall be to Me a Son'" (Hebrews 1:5).

In verse 13 of Hebrews 1 He proclaims the Messiah's authority to have dominion over all creation when He says, "Sit at My right hand, till I make Your enemies Your footstool." There was most definitely a very special bond between the Father and His only begotten, just as there was between the Creator and His first human creation.

And as God created a body for Adam to live in while relating to the natural world, so He gave Jesus a body to live in while doing the same. Again, Hebrews tells us, in speaking of Jesus's relation to the Father, "A body You have prepared for Me" (10:5).

This is one of the many wonderful miracles our God performed to enable His Son to perfectly relate to the humans He came to save. The writer of Hebrews once again gives us help in understanding this amazing truth when he says, "Therefore, in all things He *had to be made like His brethren,* that He might be a merciful and faithful High Priest in things pertaining to God, to make propitiation for the sins of the people. For in that He Himself has suffered, being tempted, He is able to aid those who are tempted" (2:17–18, emphasis added).

He further states in chapter 4, verse 15, "We do not have a High Priest who cannot sympathize with our weaknesses, but was in all points tempted as we are, yet without sin."

The apostle Paul echoes this truth in his letter to the Philippians when he writes, "[Jesus] made Himself of no reputation, taking the form of a bondservant, and coming in *the likeness of men.* And being found *in appearance as a man,* He humbled Himself and became obedient to the point of death, even the death of the cross" (2:7–8, emphasis added).

By creating a body for Christ to dwell in, the Father enabled His Son to perfectly relate to humanity. We are not alone in our sufferings and sorrows. Our loneliness, hurt, depression, even our anger and fear are felt and understood by the Father through His incarnate Son! Hallelujah—what a Savior!

Also, the love returned to the Father from the Son is the love that God desired from Adam. In Psalm 40:8 the preincarnate Christ is speaking when He says, "I delight to do Your will, O my God, and Your law is within my heart." What kind of world might we live in today if Adam had said those same words and had the same mind?

There is another similarity between the two Adams, the two representatives of humanity. The first Adam was created with the ability to fill the earth with a people who would receive and forward the love of God. In Genesis 1:28 we read, "Then God blessed them, and God said to them, 'Be fruitful and multiply; fill the earth and subdue it; have dominion over the fish of the sea, over the birds of the air, and over every living thing that moves on the earth.'"

As Adam was to fill the earth with mini-Me's, so Jesus came to fill the earth with a people who would rule as kings and queens in God's kingdom. John the Revelator makes this clear when he writes, "To Him who loved us and washed us from our sins in His own blood, and *has made us kings and priests* to His God and Father, to Him be glory and dominion forever and ever. Amen" (Revelation 1:5–6, emphasis added).

Jesus himself, said, "Do not fear, little flock, for it is your Father's good pleasure to give you the kingdom" (Luke 12:32). Believers have the authority to subdue the enemy at every turn. Each time the enemy attacks, we must remember that we are more than conquerors because of the Spirit of Christ within us. It is not our strength or power but

His that enables us to rise above the challenges of life. And as someone has said, "Life is what happens when you make plans."

Out of the Spirit and the mouth of Christ He said to us "Behold, I give you the authority to trample on serpents and scorpions, and over all the power of the enemy, and nothing shall by any means hurt you" (Luke 10:19). If we believers would truly believe who we are in Christ, we would subdue the evil that attempts to steal our joy and peace. We would also be aiding in setting other captives free to enjoy God's love and blessing. The stumbling blocks would actually become stepping stones if only we would take God at His word. If only . . .

If we will take God at His word, we can all be Adams. It is God's purpose to have us subdue the earth and have dominion over it. It is His will that we be fruitful and multiply. God is inviting us to partner with Him in being good stewards of His creation. To do this He gave Adam a body, a soul, and a spirit. Adam was and all humans are a trichotomy, three persons in one, created in the image of God. We are each a spirit with a soul that lives in a body.

The body is how we relate to the world around us. It is the machine that brings us visual images, sounds, smells, tastes, and touch. The soul and spirit process and interpret these senses. The body, then, is the vehicle to take our spirit and soul wherever the next challenge arises or the next need exists. When the enemy comes in like a flood, the spirit takes the lead by connecting with God and listening to His plan of attack. The spirit then sends the message to the soul to tell us what to speak to the enemy. The word spoken goes forward as a prayer to God or by command to the intruder.

It is helpful in this area to understand that there is a chain of command. The chain begins with God the Father. He sent His Son, who sent His Holy Spirit. His Spirit communicates with the spirit of humanity. Humanity's spirit has authority over the soul, which is our mind, will, and emotions. The soul is to rule over the body, which is low man on the totem pole. The Father is the commander-in-chief while the body is the private. The body is still important in that it is the vehicle that puts into action the commands given to it by the spirit and to the soul.

This is because our weapons are not carnal—they are spiritual. The battle is won by prayer, fasting, and obedience to the will of God. The battle isn't even our battle—it is the Lord's—but He works in and through us to win the victory. The tempter used humans as his weapon against God in the garden. God uses the same tactic. He uses humans who are filled with the Spirit to overcome the power of the enemy. The commander-in-chief has turned the tables on Satan by using his own strategy against him.

In this modern garden, however, we have different challenges to subdue than did Adam and Eve. We have a roaring lion who uses diseases, disasters, and devils in an attempt to destroy us. The first Adam had a devil to defeat also. Unfortunately, he did not accomplish the work. The last Adam had a devil to defeat and rose above and beyond the challenge. Jesus has given His followers the authority and power to do the same thing. And in the modern garden Jesus has shown us how to do it.

While in a human body Jesus gave us many visual aids on fighting the good fight. These aids were "training films" for using body, soul, and spirit to defeat the enemy. One of these aids was His temptation in the wilderness. Immediately after His baptism, described in Mark 1, the Holy Bible tells us that the Spirit drove Jesus into the wilderness for the express purpose of being tempted by the devil.

As Christ was being tempted, the Spirit planned Satan's defeat by sending the message to the mind of Christ that God was faithful and His word was true. There would be a victorious conclusion to this battle. The mind of Christ transmitted the plan to His tongue and the words were spoken through His mouth: "It is written," "It is written," "It is written (Matthew 4:1–10).

The battle wasn't won with sword or spear. It was won by words—words put into action by faith, words that did not return void but accomplished what they were sent to do. The weapons that His body used to defeat the enemy were words! Rather than being snared by the words of His mouth (Proverbs 6:2), Jesus was delivered by the words of His mouth. He knew beyond all doubt that the words of His Father were unshakeable and unchangeable. Jesus withstood the temptations with a full frontal attack. His Spirit planned the attack, His soul transmitted the plan, and His body carried it out.

In that training film the battle was won because of the last Adam's determined trust in the Father. A few short years later, Jesus would again trust God when, on the cross, He said, "Father, 'into Your hands I commit My spirit'" (Luke 23:46). Unwavering trust, unshakeable faith—these are the weapons to use in keeping the body in subjection to the spirit. The body is an incredibly complex machine. It is "fearfully and wonderfully made" (Psalm 139:14).

In Romans 12:1 Paul instructed us to present our bodies to God as a living sacrifice. When we do so, the body can be a powerful tool to carry out God's plan of attack through the spirit and soul. The last Adam taught us how to do just that. The last Adam taught us well.

Adam, red earth—the revelation that Christ lived in a body. He was physical like us. He had feelings like us. He even felt pain like us. He ran the gamut of human suffering and won! Where the first Adam failed the last Adam prevailed.

2

CAIN:
Man of Death

The two brothers, Cain and Abel, possibly twins, don't figure into the lineage of Christ or into the Begatitudes, the reason being that Abel was murdered and Cain was banished. The meanings of their names, however, are still important.

We will begin with Cain, whose name means "lance" or "spear." It relates, of course, to one of the weapons that figured prominently in the death of Christ. The spear did not actually kill the Messiah, but it was used to prove that He was indeed dead. And even though we are not told what weapon Cain used to kill his brother, *Kah'-yin* is an astonishingly unique way of foretelling that a spear would be involved. And our God is certainly unique! Or as we might say, "He is one of a kind."

Cain further sets a societal example for us in that we should learn that a spear, or any other weapon, is not an acceptable way to settle our differences. There are good uses for a spear, such as hunting or defending one's family and property. To raise it in anger toward a fellow human or for vengeance against him or her is not the proper way to use this tool.

Another lesson that can be learned from Cain has little to do with the name but is nevertheless an important truth. The lesson is that the very first murder in human history was due to religious persecution. In Hebrews 11:4 we read, "By faith Abel offered to God a more excellent sacrifice than Cain, through which he obtained witness that he was righteous, God testifying of his gifts; and through it he being dead still speaks."

Cain was jealous because Abel's sacrifice was accepted by Yahweh—even though He said to Cain, "Why are you angry? And why has your countenance fallen? If you do well, will you not be accepted? And if you do not do well, sin lies at the door. And its desire is for you, but you should rule over it" (Genesis 4:6–7).

That we should do well to heed the advice and counsel of the Almighty is an understatement. Doing well wasn't for Cain alone. The Holy Bible tells us that God only wants our obedience—and obedience, by the way, that is for our own good. Obedience is not a mindless action done because we fear the consequences of disobedience. Obedience is the act of showing a loving trust in the one who asks us to obey. Our obedience is our salvation and protection.

In the Old Testament faith in God was displayed in obedience to the law. Observing the feasts, sacrifices, and commandments was proof of one's trust in God. The problem arose when the observances became their salvation rather than faith in the God who provided the salvation. They believed that keeping the law was the way to be saved. It would be somewhat like a person today saying, "I go to church—that proves I am saved." Paul spoke of this when he said that we are to live by the spirit of the law, not by the letter, because, as 2 Corinthians 3:6 says, "The letter kills, but the Spirit gives life."

A person can grit his or her teeth and clench his or her fists in the determination to be good. And in this vain attempt to be good, the person believes he or she is pleasing God and will be judged worthy of the kingdom of heaven. The psalmist David put this belief to rest when he cried out, "Have mercy upon me, O God, According to Your lovingkindness; According to the multitude of Your tender mercies, blot out my transgressions" (Psalm 51:1).

One is not saved because of doing good works—one does good works because he or she is saved! Believers become generous givers because our God is the generous giver! He gave His best and He gave His all. Believers do the same because we want to be like our Father, not because we are trying to score "points" with Him. Even if an unbeliever's good deeds outweigh the bad deeds, he or she is still lost. Only by receiving God's gift of eternal life in Jesus Christ is a sinner redeemed and made worthy to enter the Lord's kingdom. Jesus called it being "born again."

The persecution comes when believers make the bold claim that there is only one person who ever totally pleased God. There is only one person to whom God ever said, "This is My beloved Son, in whom I am well pleased. Hear Him!" (Matthew 17:5). We can safely say that God is not pleased with us no matter how many good works we do, no matter how many commandments we keep or how many sacrifices we make. He is pleased with His Son. When His Son dwells in us through the presence of the

Holy Spirit, God is pleased with my choice and accepts me as an adopted son. A friend of Jesus is a friend of mine, says the Almighty!

Unbelievers have been and will forever be trying to discount this truth. They believe the lie that they can be God. In order to do this, however, they must first do away with the one true God. This leads to the mockery and persecution of those who have genuinely put their trust in the only source of salvation, Yeshua Ha Mashiyach. If they hated the Master, they will surely hate His followers.

The choice of Cain to murder his brother, Abel, is a grim reminder that religious persecution has been around since the beginning. It will likely be around until the end. It was religious persecution that put Jesus on the cross. Granted, He laid down His life in obedience to the Father, but it was the hatred of the Jewish religious leaders that put the plan into action. Persecution led to the spear being used to verify Jesus's death.

Cain's action against Abel can also be seen as a manifestation of the spirit of antichrist. As we will see in the next chapter, Abel was a righteous man. In Cain was a spirit of jealousy and envy toward his brother. Cain hated that he could not please God with his self-righteous works. He further hated that Abel's meek and gentle spirit was accepted by Yahweh. The same spirit that was in Cain was in the people who cried out for Jesus to be crucified. The cry was started by the Pharisees and religious leaders who were jealous of Jesus and envious of the way in which the common people followed Him. They were led by the spirit of antichrist.

The Pharisees, then, became the head of the "spear" that goaded the Messiah to the cross and verified His death as He breathed His last. Just as Cain murdered an innocent and righteous man, so the Jewish leaders led a rebellion against Jesus, which led to the murder of another innocent and righteous man (Acts 5:30).

The spirit of antichrist has been in the world for much longer than most of us realize. Long before Jesus came into the world, there was a hatred for that which is pure and holy and different. Cain, the spear, certainly revealed that hatred.

For his treachery, a mark was put on Cain that caused him to stand out among his neighbors. There have been some speculations about what that mark might have been. None seem worth pursuing because they are just that: speculations. No one really knows. God did not deem it to be of great importance. He just wants us to know that Cain was branded in some way. He would be recognized as the one who murdered his own brother.

This is not a support of anti-Semitism—the Jews are no more guilty of murdering the Messiah than anyone else. This is the way it plays out: "All have sinned, and come short of the glory of God" (Romans 3:23, KJV). "The wages of sin is death" (Romans 6:23). Jesus came to "give His life a ransom for many" (Mark 10:45). His death paid the penalty of sin for all humanity. When Christ died, all died (2 Corinthians 5:14). Jesus had to die. It was the only way the debt could be settled. The Jewish people were an instrument that was used to carry out God's purpose.

Nevertheless, the Jewish religious leaders who led the charge to kill the Christ caused a mark to be put on the Jewish people. God did not put it there; rather, they put the mark on themselves. When Pilate gave in to the will of the people to crucify Jesus, he told them that he was innocent of this just man's blood. The people responded by saying, "His blood be on us and on our children" (Matthew 27:25).

There are hardly words to describe the horror of that statement. Sometimes we make statements so shocking that we immediately want to cut our tongues off. There is a lesson here. Once words are spoken, they cannot be taken back. Apologies can be made. Great sorrow may be expressed. Forgiveness may be granted. The words, however, will linger in the mind till death do us part. We try to forget, but the memory remains. Be careful, little ears, what you hear, but be even more careful, big mouth, what you say. Two ears, one mouth. Maybe we should listen twice as much as we talk.

The crowd that day talked. They talked too much. They made a damnable statement and could not take it back. It put a mark on them. The enemy has amped up his attack on God's chosen people ever since that fateful day. They have suffered immeasurably throughout the centuries. Holocausts, pogroms, exiles, and ejections have been their lot. Still God has blessed them. He will continue to do so—not because of their goodness or innocence but because of His wondrous love.

Emotions ran high that day. Words were spoken by adults that will haunt their children until the end of history. Can we learn from the experiences of others? Must we commit a crime to find out what the punishment is? In this case maybe we can learn from their horrible mistake. "Never miss a good opportunity to shut up!"— sounds flippant, but it would appear to be good advice. "Think before you speak" might be a gentler way to say it. Either way, learn a lesson from Cain. Don't be marked for shame and pain by your words or your actions. And don't be the spear that is used in vengeance toward a fellow human. If you do well, will you not be accepted?

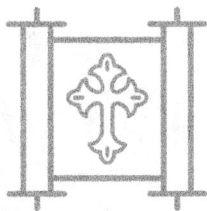

◇◇

3

ABEL:

Man of Brevity

In this chapter the name of the second man who was taken out of the Begatitudes will be recognized. The very fact that Abel was murdered at a young age makes his life as the Messiah's. Amazingly, however, it is the meaning of his name that makes his account so special among the names of these other patriarchs. Remember that Abel, as well as Cain, was named long before the meanings came to light as an important part of salvation history. It is unlikely that each person knew the uniqueness of his own name or that of his begotten.

From the Hebrew his name is *Heh'-bel*. It means "breath." The root word, however, is *ha-bal,* meaning "vanity or emptiness." It refers to something that is temporary or transitory. In other words, Abel's life, like that of Messiah's, was as short as a breath of air. Isaiah prophesies of this brevity in Isaiah 53:8 when he says of the Savior, "Who will declare His generation? For He was cut off from the land of the living."

The term *cut off* in Isaiah's prophecy is the word *gaw-zar.* It means "excluded" or "snatched away." The implication is that Jesus would not live to a ripe old age, just as the name *Abel* suggests. Jesus's earthly life was brief and to the point. He accomplished the Father's work and in a very short time taught His followers to carry it forward.

It can be said that Abel did the same thing. His name and his life teach us to be about our Father's business with humility and determination. And even though he did not live out the fullness of his years, Abel is found in the hall of faith of Hebrews 11: "By faith Abel offered to God a more excellent sacrifice than Cain, through which he obtained witness that he was righteous, God testifying of his gifts; and *through it he being dead still speaks*" (verse 4, emphasis added).

Abel's name and life are a testimony to us that God is not concerned about how long we stay on this earth. In fact, He says that the death of His saints is precious in His sight (Psalm 116:15). Whether we remain here for a short time or a long time, our

Father is glad to see us come home. He is concerned, however, with the way we spend our time while we are here! May we live as Abel, and as we are instructed by Paul in Ephesians 5:16, "Redeeming the time, because the days are evil."

Though it was cut short, Abel's life made a difference—a difference for the good of humanity. He will always be remembered as the brother whose offering pleased God. And it wasn't the sacrifice itself that was pleasing—it was Abel's attitude. He had an attitude of gratitude. It could be said that he was humbly grateful rather than grumbly hateful. The latter describes Cain's attitude. It's a choice.

A quote from Dr. Seuss comes to mind at this juncture: "Why do you want to fit in when you were born to stand out?" In other words, why do you want to just get by when your life can be a game-changer for family, friends, and society—no matter whether it's short or long? Some folk seem to want just enough salvation to get to heaven, a little fire insurance. There is so much more to being saved than just getting to heaven. A noble goal, but why not make a difference in your world while enjoying the journey home? God did not create us to barely make it. He created us just a little lower than the angels (Psalm 8:5). Believers are the King's kids. Maybe if we started believing that, we would each live with a spring in our step, a song in our heart, and a smile on our face. People will begin to wonder what we're up to when they see that kind of swagger.

Of course, the supreme example of a life making a difference is Jesus. Even though His life was as a breath, He made a difference that still wreaks havoc on the kingdom of darkness some two thousand years later. He came into Satan's darkness and left light behind. He wrestled with prejudice and hate and left love behind. He came into a prison and left behind freedom. We can't make a difference on the scale that Jesus did, but a little good is better than no good. Will we light a candle or curse the darkness? It's a choice.

There was a movement some years ago called "women's liberation." You need not look any further than God's own Son to see the great women's liberator. A woman agreed to partner with God to bring Messiah into the world (Luke 1:38). A woman blessed Jesus when He was eight days old (Luke 2:36–38). A woman washed His feet with her tears and dried them with her hair (Luke 7:38)! A woman was the first one to arrive at the empty tomb (Matthew 28:1). Jesus came to make a difference in the lives of those of the gender who had been regarded as second-class citizens. He succeeded. In His world women were not property to be bought and sold at will. They were valuable. They were important. In Jesus's world today they are still.

Even in some parts of the modern world women are considered a commodity. The pornography industry makes millions, probably billions, of dollars each year by degrading women. Young girls are kidnapped and forced into lives of prostitution. Much attention has been given lately to the equal-pay-for-equal-work movement. Motherhood is looked upon by some as an unfulfilling occupation. Women are looked down on if they don't have a career outside the home. These and many other ways reflect an attitude that women are still seen as second class. Jesus says a resounding "No!"

A particular denomination (that shall remain name-less) likely owes its very existence to the women of its churches. If women had not stepped up to head mission societies, teach Sunday school classes, and be good stewards of their resources, that particular denomination might not have survived. Jesus lifted women up to a level they had not known previously. He gave them dignity, respect, and worth. He has not discontinued that practice.

Jesus called fishermen and a tax collector to be among His disciples. He gave them dignity, respect, and worth too. They turned the world upside down because somebody made a difference in their lives. And that same somebody taught them that their lives could make a difference. Every believer has the ability to make a positive difference in the world in which he or she lives. The resource is Christ! If you are born again, you already have what you need. The intellect, the talent, the motivation are all present with every believer in the presence of the Holy Spirit. The biblical and historical examples are endless. Moses, Joshua, Rahab, Abraham and Sarah, Gideon. You do the math. Stop for a moment and think of those who have impacted your life. Some did not live long, but their life made a difference in yours. Now go and do likewise. Don't settle for mediocrity when you can have *meteorocrity*. No, it isn't a word—well, it is for now.

Abel's breath made a difference. The brevity of his life didn't matter to God. That should be a reminder that the work we are called to do is not of our intellect or in our strength. The work is God's work. We are His instruments to use at He pleases to complete His work. No one praises the hammer or the saw for building the house—at least no one in his or her right mind. No one expects the hammer or the saw to build the house. The one who builds the house is the carpenter. Think about it.

When we offer ourselves to God as willing vessels in His hands, He is pleased to bless us. When we try to do good works to please Him, He is not willing to bless us. Jesus's mother, Mary, was mentioned in a paragraph above. May we all have a spirit like Mary's. Was she aware of the difference her life was going to make when she said, "Behold the maidservant of the Lord! Let it be to me according to your word" (Luke 1:38)? There is only one word for that measure of trust, faith, and confidence: *Wow!*

Don't forget that Mary was only a teenager. She did not have years of experience and wisdom on her side. But much like Abel, her life belonged to the Lord. In a sense you might say that her life, too, ended at an early age. Not in a physical way, of course, but her focus turned away from self and toward the will of the Almighty. Paul said, "You were bought at a price" (1 Corinthians 7:23). It may be difficult to comprehend, but our lives really don't belong to us. We desperately try to make them our own, but in reality we belong to Christ. He has the right to do with us as He pleases.

Isaiah is another who offered himself to the Lord. When God wanted someone to deliver His message, Isaiah said, "Here am I! Send me" (6:8). Isaiah was a priest. He was doing an important work. In fact, he was doing a work that was ordained by God himself. That's some pretty important work! And yet he was willing to lay it aside to go forth in the name of and to the glory of God. Is that not the spirit of Abel, the spirit of doing well and being accepted—even if our lives are cut short because of that spirit?

Some will say, "I have to survive, don't I?" Do you? What is surviving if you have no future? What is living without the life of Christ? It is existence, not life. No one said it was easy. Jesus even went further than that. He said it is impossible! Only by His Spirit can we live a life surrendered to Him. And there is the key. "Whoever desires to save his life will lose it, but whoever loses his life for My sake will find it" (Matthew 16:25).

As God said to Zerubbabel, "Not by might nor by power, but by My Spirit" (Zechariah 4:6). Nothing good is accomplished in this world apart from the Spirit of God. Abel accomplished much good in his life and continues to set the example today. His was a short life, as was the life of Jesus. Abel's life was also one of humility and meekness, as was Messiah's.

Much can be learned from righteous Abel. One of those lessons is that a brief life is not necessarily a wasted life. The brevity of the life of Jesus in no way discounts the impact He had in history and in the salvation of humanity. What an understatement! But the point is that much can be accomplished by a life that is totally given over to the will of God regardless of how short the time spent on earth was.

As spoken by that great mountain-man-turned-millionaire Mr. J. D. Clampett, "Time's a'wastin'!" Whatever time we have on this earth, let's not waste it.

Brief doesn't have to mean "noneventful" or "nothing accomplished." So what are we waiting for?

4

SETH:

Man for Man

The third son of Adam is named *Shayth*, or as it is spelled in English, *Seth*, meaning "in place of" or "substitute." He took the place of the murdered Abel and the banished Cain. Seth's birth and life repaired the broken link in the chain between Adam and Noah. Eve said of her third son, "God has appointed another seed for me instead of Abel, whom Cain killed" (Genesis 4:25).

The similarity to Christ is immediately recognizable. He took our place on the cross and repaired the broken link in the chain between Yahweh and the human race. Ah, the unsearchable riches of our loving creator! No sooner is there a schism between us and our Father than He makes the way for it to be repaired.

In 2 Samuel 14 is a beautiful story of Joab sending a woman to King David with a manufactured story about her son being banished because of a fight he had with his brother. Unfortunately the brother was killed in the scuffle and the rest of the family is crying out for vengeance.

The woman tells the king that she is a widow and that her remaining son is her only means of support. She begs the king to protect him and bring him back safely from his banishment. To this request the king agrees. The award-winning actress then asks the king why he does not bring his banished son, Absalom, back into the family. This, of course, was all Joab's idea and works perfectly. David consents to bring Absalom back home.

While pleading her case, the woman makes a startling prophecy and proclamation. In 2 Samuel 14:14 she says, "We will surely die and become like water spilled on the ground, which cannot be gathered up again. Yet God does not take away a life; but He devises means, so that His banished ones are not expelled from Him."

The word *expelled* means "to drive out forcefully." Adam and Eve were expelled from the garden. It implies the action of making a person an outcast, one who has no home or family, someone who spends his or her life wandering from place to place in a futile search for peace and comfort. It further implies imposing a life of sorrow, shame, and hopelessness—much as humanity is without a relationship with its creator.

In the naming of Seth, our Father is revealing the means He has devised to bring His banished ones back to Him. It is, of course, in sending His only begotten Son to take our place by taking the punishment for our sins! Yeshua is our substitute. He is our Seth.

When our first parents sinned in the garden by calling God a liar (that's painfully difficult to write, but that is exactly what they did when they heeded the devil's voice rather than obey God), they were banished from Eden. But even as they were being cast out, Yahweh told them that not all was lost. He was making a way where there was no way. He had already devised a way to bring us back to the garden.

We are not there yet. The garden is still before us. Eventually, though, all will be restored, all will be made new, and we will once again dwell in a garden created for us by the God who loves us and gave himself for us. His banished ones need not be permanently expelled. God has devised a way to bring us home. Our substitute, the one who took our place and took our sins, has made it all possible. According to His tender mercies He has blotted out our transgressions. The Way has made the way for us to return to a life of intimate fellowship with God the Father. It begins when we are saved but will be fully seen and understood when we all get to heaven.

Jesus put it this way: "Let not your heart be troubled; you believe in God, believe also in Me. In My Father's house are many mansions; if it were not so, I would have told you. I go to prepare a place for you. And if I go and prepare a place for you, I will come again and receive you to Myself; that where I am, there you may be also" (John 14:1–3).

There is another, perhaps more familiar, story in the Old Testament that sheds light on Jesus's taking our place and being our substitute. It is the story of Abraham being called to sacrifice his son Isaac. The entire account can be found in Genesis 22.

As you know, Abraham was about to accomplish the heart-wrenching task of offering Isaac as a sacrifice when the angel of the Lord called to him not to proceed with the test. Abraham may have been a bit bewildered, but it was likely a happy bewilderment. He had already told

Isaac that God would provide a sacrifice. He did not know *how* God would provide, but Abraham did know that God would be true to His word.

This amazing story of faith, trust, and confidence in God comes to a conclusion with Abraham's seeing "a ram caught in a thicket by its horns. So Abraham went and took the ram, and offered it up for a burnt offering *instead of his son*" (Genesis 22:13, emphasis added). The ram is the substitute for Isaac just as Jesus was the substitute for humanity. The ram was another visual aid to help us understand why Adam's third son was named Seth.

Seth was the son given to Adam and Eve to take the place of the two sons who had been taken from them. It was truly a case of a man for a man. Jesus was the Son given to Adam and Eve and all their offspring to take the place of those who had been taken from their Father. Because of the Son's faithfulness to and trust in His Father's will, all humanity has the opportunity to return to an intimate relationship with God.

A brief word must be said here about Isaac also. He was a willing sacrifice. He was old enough to resist Abraham's efforts. Surely he knew what was about to happen when his father began binding him to the altar.

At his age Isaac had probably observed a few animal sacrifices and knew that a burnt offering meant death to the animal. The faith he had in Abraham is mind-boggling. What kind of person lays down voluntarily, believing that he will not rise up again? What kind of son has that kind of total abandonment to the will of his father?

The answer is clear in the words of Jesus: "No one takes it [My life] from Me, but I lay it down of Myself. I have power to lay it down, and I have power to take it again. This command I have received from My Father" (John 10:18). Jesus, the Son, knew who He was and why He had come to earth. He knew He was loved and that the Father would provide for Him. Isaac is also a foreshadow of Christ. The Holy Bible is full of hints of and allusions to the Messiah.

It cannot be over emphasized that there is nothing any person can do to save himself or herself from the wrath to come. There is no spark of good in any of us. We cannot pull ourselves up by our own bootstraps. We are hopelessly and helplessly lost. But, God . . . ! Fill in the blank. But God refused to let us go. But God saw our chains and sent a deliverer. But God heard our pitiful cry for help and came to our rescue. But God knew we had to die for our sin and He gave us a substitute, one to take our place. Jesus, the righteous one, became sin for us that we might become the righteousness of God in Him (2 Corinthians 5:21).

Believers speak of being saved by the blood of Jesus, saved from the punishment our sins, saved from an eternity of being separated from the love of God. What does all this really mean? What it boils down to is that our substitute saved us from the wrath of God! Yes, His anger will be poured out on all sin. God hates sin, not the sinner. If He hated the sinner He would not have sent His Son.

Through Christ the Father is giving us the opportunity to put our sin on Him and let Him take our punishment for us. It is truly an amazing act of selfless love. God has put our sin on His Son and we walk away free! He takes our punishment, the wrath of God, and we enjoy a blessed relationship with our creator. We are living in the day of God's amazing grace.

After the close of the war in Vietnam some people began asking what would happen to those who had fled the country to avoid the draft. The answer was given when the powers that be declared a time of amnesty for them. The assertion was that they could return to America with a full pardon! Their crimes would be forgiven and forgotten. There was a stipulation, however: they had to return within a certain period of time. Amnesty would not last forever. The door to forgiveness and freedom would stand open for only a short time.

What possible reason would a person have for turning down such an incredible offer of redemption? Yet there were likely some who did just that. Did they think it was a trick? Did they think the government leaders were lying? (Imagine that.) For whatever reason, some did not take advantage of this most generous offer.

This is what our Seth did for us. He took our place on the cross, died for our sins, and now offers us amnesty. "Just come home!" is the cry of the Father's heart. No questions asked. No judgment rendered. After all, He already knows where we have been and what we have done. But His grace, His amnesty only wants us to return to the fold.

The ultimate story to illustrate this truth is what we refer to as that of "the prodigal son." A wealthy father was looking for his son to return home. When he saw his son far off, he ran to meet him. That was something, by the way, that wealthy and dignified men did not do. They walked slowly so everyone could admire them. The prodigal's father didn't care about being admired—he cared about his son! Even when his son tried to confess his crimes and take a lowly position in the family, the father would have none of it. He welcomed him back into the family as if he had never left! He treated him to clean clothes, new shoes, the family seal, and a shindig! The words of Jesus rang true: "I say to you, there is joy in the presence of the angels of God over one sinner who repents" (Luke 15:10).

This day of God's amnesty will not last forever. As the door to Noah's ark was eventually shut, so will the door to everlasting joy and peace. And don't forget who shut the door to the ark. To refresh your memory, see Genesis 7:16. Only God knows when this door of grace will be shut. Why would anyone reject such an incredible offer of forgiveness and freedom?

Sometimes we refer to people who have escaped punishment for a crime by saying, "They got away with murder." So, my friend, did every one of us who has accepted God's forgiveness and received His gift of eternal life! Not only did we get away with murder—we also got away with lying, cheating, stealing and more. And now Jesus instructs us to go and sin no more. The apostle Paul puts it like this: "Let him who stole steal no longer, but rather let him labor, working with his hands what is good, that he may have something to give him who has need" (Ephesians 4:28).

Spiritually speaking, we are to rejoice in our newfound freedom not only for ourselves—we are also to help others find the same freedom, to escape the wrath of God by living a life that glorifies Him and directing others to His saving grace. In that way believers can be likened to substitutes also. We are little "Seths," substitutes for the physical presence of Christ in the world. "We are ambassadors for Christ, as though God were pleading through us: we implore you on Christ's behalf, be reconciled to God" (2 Corinthians 5:20).

To illustrate this, imagine that you have a cup that has been so deeply tainted with the stains of tea and coffee that it is impossible to clean. No matter how you scrub the cup, the stains just won't come off. You finally decide to throw the cup away and get a new one. As you are walking toward the trash can, someone tells you of a wonderful new product that will remove those stains— it's called "bleach." You apply the bleach to the stains, and *voila!*—they disappear. Would you not be quick and persistent in telling others about this amazing stain-removing product?

There is another facet to this stain remover. With the stains gone, the cup is spared from the trash heap and is put to good use again. Just so, the penalty for our sins was paid when God put them on our substitute. Our "cup" has been cleansed and we are now made fit for God to use us as testimonials of His great love. This is not meant flippantly or casually, but in the previous illustration the blood of Jesus is the "bleach" that cleanses us from all unrighteousness.

What can wash away my sin? You know the answer. Nothing—but the blood of Jesus. Next question: What can make me whole again? Same answer. Next question, same answer. In these last days God has one word for all that ails us: *Yeshua*. He came to our world so we could come to His. He became like us so we could become like Him. He gave His life to redeem ours. That is an incredible exchange by an amazing substitute! May He always be your *Seth*.

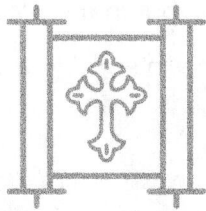

5

ENOSH:

Man of Flesh

Enosh simply means "man." (This may be a short chapter.) The deeper meaning is implied in the fact that our Savior was completely man at the same time He was completely God. Yes, a strange mixture indeed, somewhat like trying to mix oil and water. And yet with God all things are possible and there is nothing impossible for Him. So the combination worked. It worked perfectly. Jesus was the perfect God-man.

Through His deity He was able to reach out to His heavenly Father. Through His humanity He was able to reach out to His earthly family (Matthew 12:47–49). It was truly the only way to solve the dilemma of saving humanity while saving face.

In this chapter the focus is on the human aspect of Christ. After all, *Enosh,* once again, means "man." Christ was the only one who could sacrifice His life for the salvation of humanity (Revelation 5:2–10).

Here is the problem: through the prophet Ezekiel God had said, "The soul who sins shall die" (18:20). Actually He began with Adam, when God told him that he would die if he disobeyed the command not to eat of the tree of the knowledge of good and evil. But He made it more specific when He spoke through Ezekiel.

Since all have sinned, what can this mean except that every soul has to pay the penalty for sin, which is death? But the heart of God was set on having a people He could love and bless. If every person pays for his or her sin, then every person dies. That doesn't leave anyone to love outside the Trinity.

And since a man betrayed humanity, the only solution was that a man redeem humanity. The problem? There was no perfectly obedient, perfectly sinless man. As Adam had represented all humanity and each of us has inherited that fallen nature, it was needful that another man represent humanity with a sinless nature.

How could this be? How could one person represent all of humanity? It is a poor illustration, but it might help to imagine the human race as a football team. It makes it a bit more difficult to imagine when no one had been born to our first parents at the time they were representing us!

At the time of their innocence, however, every soul was in the bodies of Adam and Eve. They were our original parents; therefore, all humanity came from them. All of us can trace our existence back to them. So humanity is a football team. The team elects a captain to go to the center of the field before the start of the game to meet the other team's captain and take part in the coin toss. The captain of the opposing team, of course, is Satan. The captain of our team, Adam, chooses "heads" and the coin lands on "tails." We lose. Our captain made the wrong choice. In reality he chose to believe Lucifer's lie rather than God's truth. But for now let's stick to the analogy of the football team.

No one on our team can say, "But I didn't get to call which side the coin landed on. I don't like the way the toss ended." Oh, well. Our captain was chosen to make the call for us. Good or bad, we now must play the game by our captain's choice. Adam, our captain, made a bad choice—an unspeakably bad choice. He made a choice so bad, so selfish, so destructive that it sent the whole human race and all of creation into a tailspin.

The creation that we experience now most certainly does not possess the beauty, purity, and peace that was given to us in the beginning. If it did, Paul would not say, "For the earnest expectation of the creation eagerly waits for the revealing of the sons of God. For the creation was subjected to futility, not willingly, but because of Him who subjected it in hope; because the creation itself also will be delivered from the bondage of corruption into the glorious liberty of the children of God. For we know that the whole creation groans and labors with birth pangs together until now" (Romans 8:19–22).

The first Adam brought wreck and ruin into God's perfect world. And as an aside, here, let no one be judgmental toward Adam. Some might think they will chastise him when they see him in heaven. Others might just want to ask him why he took Eve's side instead of God's (a question most men can readily answer, but that's a subject for another book). They may want to ask how in the world he could have believed Satan rather than God.

Before we condemn Adam, we must every one ask, "What would I have done if I had been the first human and were given the same choice?" If we are honest, we will admit that we would be in this same predicament no matter who made the choice. His name might have been *Allen, Aaron,* or *Aesop*—and the result would have been the same. In other words, we have all sinned and come short of the glory of God. If it hadn't been Adam, it would have been you or me, whatever your name may be. We have all chosen to be our own gods at one time or another. Anytime we don't obey the promptings and leadings of the Holy Spirit, we are making the wrong choice once again. Disobedience is a statement that we fancy ourselves to be smarter than our creator. Disobedience says that we know how to take care of ourselves better than our God does.

So our first captain didn't make a good call. As was said earlier, this did not catch God off guard. He didn't wring His hands and wonder what to do. He didn't grab His playbook and hastily try to come up with another call. There was no plan A and plan B. There was only a plan A. Our last captain had been on the team all along and was waiting His turn to get in the game. Yes, the football illustration seems shallow, but Jesus was a master at using physical events to explain spiritual truths. Hopefully this analogy will do the same thing.

After Adam's sin God began the task of fulfilling His promise of Genesis 3:15—"I will put enmity between you and the woman, and between your seed and her Seed; He shall bruise your head, and you shall bruise His heel." In His world of timelessness the task is finished immediately. In fact, it was done before the foundation of the world. God, however, is working in our world. The work of bringing the last Adam to us would take thousands of our earth years but would eventually come in "the fullness of time" (Galatians 4:4). Our last captain was on the way.

And He was a man—a man like us! He was a man who felt pain and sorrow as well as joy and peace. He was a man who had feelings and knew what it was like to be rejected, hated, and even feared, a man who was a hero one day and, yes, a goat the next, a man who "was in all points tempted as we are, yet without sin" (Hebrews 4:15).

Jesus was and is now the one who represents us. He, a man, was hung on a cross for us but is now seated at the right hand of the Father. And He makes intercession for us! He, a man, took every one of our sins upon himself and paid the price that we might go free. Think of it: every sin we committed was placed on Christ as if He had done it. He who knew no sin became sin. He became a murderer, a liar, a thief. Unthinkable! No wonder the Pharisees and religious leaders could not accept God's perfect plan. To them it was a scandal. God was too holy and too high to die as a common criminal. And yet that is just what He did. The law was broken by us—the debt was paid by Him.

A man betrayed us—a man redeemed us. The name, *Enosh*, is so very simple in its meaning: "man." But it is filled with meaning when it is spoken as a revelation of who Jesus was and what He did for us. Peter tells us, "Since Christ suffered for us in the flesh, arm yourselves also with the same mind, for he who has suffered in the flesh has ceased from sin" (1 Peter 4:1).

Jesus was "in the flesh" and it was in that flesh that He suffered for us. Whereas the first Adam refused to suffer, the last Adam suffered greatly. Whereas the first Adam would not obey the voice of the Lord, the last Adam, "being found in appearance as a man, He humbled Himself and became obedient to the point of death, even the death of the cross" (Philippians 2:8). As a man, a flesh-

and-blood man, a sinless man, Jesus was obedient to His Father, and in doing so He redeemed us. He thereby gave us the opportunity to have restored fellowship with the Father.

It bears repeating: the name *Enosh* teaches us that just as a man betrayed us, so a man redeemed us. The old saying is that you fight fire with fire. The wisdom and might of God did that. Not literally, but in sending His Son in the form of a man, He was the perfect one to represent the rest of the team.

There are some who don't like having Jesus as their captain. All right—that's their right. God always gives us the right to choose. There are only two teams, however. If you don't like Christ as your captain, you're surely not going to like the other one. But those are the two choices. Either Jesus represents you or Satan does. Make your choice, and let's get on with the game or the war, if you will. And never forget that God wins! That means that believers win. Don't think so? Read the back of the Book.

6

CAINAN:

Man of the House

*C*ainan, *Kay-nawn',* is one of the most difficult names to fit into the life of Jesus. It means "possession" and is from a root word, *kane,* which means a "chamber or dwelling." With this in mind, it is somewhat easier to arrive at the understanding that Christ is our possession as we are His. Add the root word to it, and it becomes clearer. Jesus is our dwelling place, a dwelling place that we possess. He isn't a rental. He isn't temporary. He is ours, as we are His. He was given as a gift from God.

In John 17:21 Jesus prays for the disciples by asking "that they also may be one in Us." He continues in verse 23 by praying, "I in them, and You in Me." This was fulfilled in the giving of the Holy Spirit. Through the presence of the Spirit, Christ dwells in us and we dwell in Him. We are washed inside and out. By dwelling in us He is cleansing the soul. By our dwelling in Him He is cleansing the body. Truly the blood of Jesus cleanses us from all unrighteousness (1 John 1:7).

Jesus washes away all our sins and even puts to death the sin nature. The sin nature is the desire, or "want to," that is part of the fallen nature. It is one thing to get rid of all our sins—it is quite another to get rid of the factory that keeps producing it. Someone once said that he would like to destroy all the cigarettes in the world—a noble work. But even if that were possible, would not the tobacco producers make more cigarettes?

The only way to get rid of cigarettes, or anything else that so easily besets us, is to get rid of the factory that produces it. So, you might ask, do we destroy all the cigarette factories? No. Again, the tobacco industry would simply build them back again. The answer if to get rid of the consumer! If there is no one to buy the product, the company goes out of business. Do we then kill all the people who smoke, dip, or chew? Do we kill all the people who watch pornography or all the people who throw away life savings at casinos and racetracks?

That is one way—to get rid of the consumer. It's a rather harsh way, however. But the same rule applies here. Would not the next generation produce more consumers? There must be a way to rid the world of sin without ridding it of people.

Getting rid of the consumer is one way to illustrate getting rid of the sin nature, the nature within us that wants to cling to sin. Maybe that's why Lot's wife looked back. She wanted to hang on to the old life. After all, there is pleasure in sin for a season. Even the mind of a born-again believer can remember the things that once brought pleasure to the flesh.

When one is born again, the forgiveness offered in Christ is accepted and the penalty of death has been paid by Christ. The factory, however, has not been put out of business. It is possible, and likely, that the heart will produce more sin. Jesus said in Matthew 15:19, "Out of the heart proceed evil thoughts, murders, adulteries, fornications, thefts, false witness, blasphemies." The heart has been cleansed of sins, but it's the sin *production* that needs to be put out of business.

How is this task accomplished? The answer is found in the Old Testament. Hundreds of years before the birth of

Christ, God said through the prophet Ezekiel, "I will give you a new heart and put a new spirit within you; I will take the heart of stone out of your flesh and give you a heart of flesh. I will put My Spirit within you and cause you to walk in My statutes, and you will keep My judgments and do them" (Ezekiel 36:26–27). Another word for "cause" in verse 27 might be "enable." In other words, God wants to give us the ability, or enable us, not to sin! It isn't to say that we *can't* sin. As long as we are in these human bodies, we will be able to sin. By the indwelling presence of the Holy Spirit, however, we are enabled to resist the temptation to sin.

There is a difference between involuntary sin and voluntary sin. By the power of the indwelling Spirit of God, every believer is able to resist voluntary sin. The factory has been put out of business because there is no longer a consumer. James explains it this way: "Each one is tempted when he is drawn away by his own desires and enticed. Then, when desire has conceived, it gives birth to sin; and sin, when it is full-grown, brings forth death" (1:14–15). By the grace of God He gives us a spirit that resists the desire to be enticed and drawn away. He replaces the "want to" with a "don't want to." Sin no longer has dominion over us. Again, we *can* sin, but we hate what God hates. And God hates that which separates us from Him.

So the question comes up time and again: Are we able to continue committing sin? Unfortunately, the answer is yes. Only by the indwelling of the Holy Spirit is any believer able to conquer the desire to sin. God prophesied this truth once again in the Old Testament when He said, "Your ears shall hear a word behind you, saying, 'This is the way, walk in it,' whenever you turn to the right hand or whenever you turn to the left" (Isaiah 30:21).

What a great name is the name *Cainan*! Because of its meaning, we understand that the Father always meant for His Son to be our possession and our dwelling place. As long as you stay in the house, you are safe from the prowling beasts of prey on the outside—especially that one that goes about as a roaring lion.

Once upon a time a man had some chickens. One evening one of the chickens would not return to the hen house. She said in her heart that she was free. She was finished being cooped up. After all, that coop was nothing more than a chicken prison. The man tried in vain for a great while to catch the chicken and put her safely into the coop. He finally gave up and the hen was left out to enjoy her "freedom." In the morning all that remained of that hen was a pile of feathers. The moral? For safety's sake, stay in the coop! It isn't a prison—it's a place of safety and security. This is our Christ, our place of safety and security.

While a believer surrenders every thought and action to the Spirit of God (2 Corinthians 10:5), he or she is safe from the "want to" of sin. When the believer leaves his or her dwelling place, there is great danger of being devoured by the enemy. The fox is always looking for a chicken who has left the safety of the coop.

When Jesus told the disciples in Mark 4 to get into the boat, He further told them in verse 35 that they were going to "cross over to the other side." He did not say that there would not be any difficulties during the crossing. He did not say that they would have smooth sailing. He simply told them that they would reach the other side of the lake.

If any of those disciples had decided to abandon ship, they probably would have died. As long as they stayed in the boat they were safe. Why? Because Jesus was in the boat! When we keep Him in our boat and keep our boat in Him, all is well. There will be storms, but Jesus is the master of the sea, the calmer of the storm. *Stay in the boat.*

There is another Old Testament example of the inward and outward cleansing that God offers to every soul. It too has to do with a boat. As we observe one aspect of this boat, remember God's passion. His Word is the history of the Father pursuing His wayward children. This passion did not come into being at the birth of Christ. It has been in the Father's heart since the beginning.

The parable of the hundred sheep is another great illustration of the Father's love. The shepherd left the ninety-nine sheep that were safe in the fold to find the one sheep that had wandered away. This parable, however, is from the New Testament and may lead some to believe that salvation in the name of Jesus was just an afterthought. It can't be emphasized enough: God's passion has always been redemption.

So we look back in the Old Testament, long before any parable told by Jesus, to the illustration of Noah's ark. A study of this big boat will reveal a great many aspects of the life of Christ. As always, God is using an earthly example to explain a heavenly truth. Get out your pick and shovel. The gold is usually beneath the surface.

The part of the ark story to focus on to illustrate that the Holy Spirit "dwells with you and will be in you" (John 14:17) is when God told Noah in Genesis 6:14, "Make yourself an ark of gopherwood; make rooms in the ark, and *cover it inside and outside with pitch*" (emphasis added). Pitch is a type of tar and was used as a sealant. It was made in this case to keep the water out and thereby keep the occupants dry, warm, and alive.

For us the pitch represents the blood of Jesus and the presence of the Holy Spirit. It is these two attributes of God that seal out sin and seal in His holiness.

The ark was God's instrument to save humanity. It was large enough to save anyone who would get on board. We know that only eight people believed God. Only eight souls were saved. That, of course, was not a failure on God's part. He did everything necessary to save humanity. As in these last days, however, few people heeded His warning.

God is doing everything necessary to save souls. He has told us, without mincing words, that His Son is our ark of safety. Only by getting into the ark are we spared from the wrath of God that is coming upon sin. And the emphasis here is that God's wrath is going to be poured out on sin. The anger of Yahweh is not toward sinners but rather toward the sin that so easily besets us. The down side is that those who have not given their sins to Christ and boarded the ark will experience the wrath of God on the sins they would not surrender to Him.

The vessel, the soul that continues to allow sin to rule in his or her mortal body will be punished along with the sin that he or she harbors. With Noah's ark God is revealing His plan to save us. The plan is that we accept Christ as our Messiah and enter the ark. Once inside, we are sealed by the blood of Jesus inside and out! It bears repeating: sin is sealed out and holiness is sealed in. The ark of Yeshua is our dwelling place. It is our possession—as the name *Cainan* implies.

It would be perfectly acceptable to refer to Jesus as "John's ark" or "Mary's ark" or by whatever other name you are known by. Christ is your ark if you are born again. You are in His boat and He has said to you, "Get in. Let's go to the other side."

7

MAHALALEL:
Man of Praise

The meaning of the name *Mahalalel* is fascinating. He is the son of Cainan, whose name reminds us that Christ is our dwelling place, our ark of safety. The firstborn son of Cainan is given a name that means "praise of/to God." Because of the Father's ark, who is now *our* ark, we have reason to praise the Lord.

It goes further. The two words from which *Mahalalel* comes, *Mah-hal-awl'* and *El,* combine to mean "Praise to God, my strength." Anytime the name *El* is seen in a person's name, it means "strength" and refers to the one who is the Almighty. For example, *Daniel* means "judge of God." The name *Ezekiel* means "God will strengthen."

Mahalalel, then, can mean "I will give praise to my God, who is my strength." This is a major theme of the Holy Bible and particularly in the Psalms, which is a hymnbook of songs of praise to God. Not only are they songs of praise, but they also inspire the singers and listeners to give praise. It is also the major theme of Jesus's life. In John 5:19 He said, "Most assuredly, I say to you, the Son can do nothing of Himself, but what He sees the Father do; for whatever He does, the Son also does in like manner." Copying someone else or, better yet, attempting to be like him or her is the greatest form of praise. Imitation is the greatest form of flattery.

The passion of the Christ is to bring sinners to repentance, and the best way to do that is to bring praise to His Father. Jesus spent His earthly life giving praise to God and acknowledging that Yahweh was His strength. Believers, too, should be about the business of making God famous.

When we begin to slightly understand the great lengths to which our Father went to redeem us, it should inspire us to give Him praise and thanks. The prophet Isaiah says that God has formed a people for himself to declare His praise (43:21). We are told that God lives in the praise of His people (Psalm 22:3). So if you want the Father's presence in your life, praise Him!

What does it mean to praise the Lord? And why does God instruct us to do it? On the surface it sounds vain. This is because we see most things through the eyes of our fallen nature. People who want praise are usually arrogant and self-centered. The story is told of two athletes who competed against one another in the game of soccer. They were both incredibly gifted and talented and vain. In an interview one said that he was so good at playing soccer that he felt that the very reason God had put him on earth was to show people how to play the game. When the other player was asked to respond to that statement, he said, "For the life of me, I can't remember sending him!" Vanity of vanities.

To understand why it is imperative that we give God praise, we must first look at life from His point of view. What does it mean to praise the Lord? Fundamentally, it means to acknowledge that He is the creator and sovereign ruler of all that exists. The Psalms, as previously mentioned, are filled with encouragements to praise God. Perhaps the one that sets the tone would be Psalm

24:1, which says, "The earth is the Lord's, and all its fullness, the world and those who dwell therein."

Since therefore God created and owns everything, even humanity, we give Him praise by simply acknowledging that truth. Every life is in God's hands. When Daniel was called in to interpret the handwriting on the wall, he told Belshazzar, "You have praised the gods of silver and gold, bronze and iron, wood and stone, which do not see or hear or know; and *the God who holds your breath in His hand and owns all your ways*, you have not glorified" (Daniel 5:23, emphasis added). Paul echoes this in Acts 17:28 when he says, "In Him we live and move and have our being."

All creation and every creature, including humanity, belong to God. He alone is responsible for giving us life. He brought us into being and bought us back when we sold ourselves to the enemy to be his slaves. He is worthy of our acknowledgment that He is the source of life itself. He owns the air we breathe, the food we eat, the clothes we wear. And these are just the physical blessings. These things are for the body. What about the soul and spirit of humanity?

There also God is sovereign. He supplies spiritual food and drink for our dead spirits and hungry souls. In Ecclesiastes 3:10–11 Solomon says, "I have seen the God-given task with which the sons of men are to be occupied. He has made everything beautiful in its time. Also He has put eternity in their hearts, except that no one can find out the work that God does from beginning to end."

Without changing the meaning of that verse, it would better read, "He has put eternity in their hearts, without which no one can find out the work that God does from beginning to end." God wants us to find out the work that He is doing. He wants us to understand the plans He has for us. So we have a God-given task with which we are to be occupied! And it isn't dwelling on the things of this world like food and drink. Yes, we acknowledge that our Father is the provider of all these necessities, but our work is to think about eternity, to ponder what God is up to.

If God had not given every person a heart to know things eternal, our lives would devolve into nothing more than being occupied with entertainment, food, and illness. We live in a CO-ED society: many people are Celebrity Obsessed and Entertainment Driven—CO-ED.

The next time you are in line at the department store or grocery store, notice the magazines strategically planted where you are sure to see them. Very nearly all, if not all, are obsessed with details about celebrities. Movie stars, music stars, political stars consume our thinking. We need to set our sights much higher.

Food is another obsession. Yes, we need it. Paul, however, gives a word to the wise when he says, "Whether you eat or drink, or whatever you do, do all to the glory of God" (1 Corinthians 10:31). Again, acknowledge that our Father, Jehovah Jireh, is the provider of all things. And food is given as a necessity to keep the body fueled, not something to be worshiped.

Take note of the programs and commercials on television that deal with food. There is even a network devoted entirely to food! There is nothing sinful about eating unless it becomes an obsession or an idol. We must eat to live, not live to eat. Food is a necessary blessing that can easily become a curse. Listen to your conversations throughout the week. How often do you talk about food, what you like and don't like, what you are having for dinner tonight or tomorrow or next week, what you had for lunch yesterday? I knew a man once who would discuss what he was going to have for dinner the next day—while he was eating dinner! Discuss the God who *gives* the food. That's why Jesus set the example in asking the Father to bless what was about to be eaten. It would probably be a good idea to offer a blessing over our food before *and* after it is eaten. That would be giving praise to God.

Another thing we are occupied with is our illnesses, sicknesses, surgeries, and medicines. Sometimes we wear these as a red badge of courage or a purple heart. At other times we play "Can you top this?" by attempting to describe a more serious illness, accident, or surgery than anyone else. Just as it is with food, there is no sin in talking about illness, especially if we are asking for prayer. The obsession comes when we take pride in sickness and it is the favorite, or only, topic of conversation.

There is a positive way to speak of our illnesses and that is to give God praise for healing and deliverance. Once again, this approach goes back to acknowledging God as the one who provides all things for us. Whether He intervened in a supernatural way or used a doctor, surgeon, or medicine, the great physician is the cure we should be bragging about.

Praising God, then, is to acknowledge that He is the provider of every good and perfect gift. If there is an obsession, let it be talking about the goodness of the Father.

The thought that follows this is that it seems a bit arrogant of God to instruct us to give Him all the glory and praise. In Isaiah God says, "I am the LORD, that is My name; And My glory I will not give to another, nor My praise to carved images" (42:8). "LORD" means that He is the self-existent one. He doesn't need air, food, entertainment, or any of the things that humans need. He lives because He lives. He can receive all the praise and glory because He doesn't need it and it won't go to His head.

With humans, no matter how saved and sanctified we may be, praise will eventually go to our head. We will pridefully begin to believe all the good things others are saying about us. This is why so many superstars have colossal egos. A person who is paid to make us think that he or she is someone else begins thinking that his or her talent is deserving of high praise. If that praise comes often enough, the person begins to believe that he or she is a god—even though his or her gift is the gift of hypocrisy! The person is paid large amounts of money to wear a mask. Think about it.

Athletes, and performers in general, are much the same way. A man can throw a baseball ninety-plus miles per hour and strike out the opposing team's batters and is praised for it. He begins thinking of himself as a superstar. Rather than thanking God for the gift, he takes all the praise on himself. He doesn't realize that it was God who formed him in his mother's womb and gave him the talents he possesses.

The list of athletes, performers, and entertainers who have great talents and correspondingly great egos is probably rather long. They come from every race, creed, and color known to humanity. They seem to be unaware that a talent is a gift and that gifts come from someone who loves them.

There is only one who can receive praise, honor, and glory and not be affected by it. His name is Yahweh, Lord of all. He is already as talented, gifted, mighty, and intelligent as He will ever be. He knows all, is all powerful, and is all present. No amount of praise can make Him think He is greater than all others. He already knows it.

But He uses His greatness to help us have a right relationship with Him. He allows us the privilege of sharing in His holiness and His blessings. And that is praiseworthy!

Mahalalel is the name to remind us of God's worthiness to receive all our praise, worship, and thanksgiving. Jesus set the tone for a lifestyle of praising God. Lead on, O Lord our strength. And give us sense enough to follow.

8

JARED:

Man Who Descended

The name *Yeh'-red* has more than one revelation in the life of Christ. *Jared* means "descent" or "to descend." The first revelation, then, should be a given. Jesus came down, or descended, from heaven to earth to save the lost. He left the beauty and purity of heaven to come into an ugly and sinful world. That is quite a steep descent.

Christ brought the presence of the Father into the world. And when one comes from heaven to earth, it is definitely a descent. James puts it this way: "Every good gift and every perfect gift is from above, and comes down from the Father of lights" (James 1:17). Yeshua was most certainly the good and perfect gift. He is the gift that has not been very well received, but all who do receive Him receive eternal life.

Jesus came down to earth as the visible image of God the Father. He was the son that He spoke of in the parable of the wicked vinedressers. The parable ends with Jesus saying, "But when the vinedressers saw the son, they said among themselves, 'This is the heir. Come, let us kill him and seize his inheritance.' So they took him and cast him out of the vineyard and killed him" (Matthew 21:38–39).

Over the centuries God had sent many ambassadors and diplomats to bring His message of love and grace to a fallen world. Each in turn had been cursed, beaten, and even murdered. In Christ, God was doing what humans often refer to this way: "If you want a job done right, you need to do it yourself." So God came down to earth in the person of Jesus the Messiah. Paul reached this conclusion when he said, "He is the image of the invisible God, the firstborn over all creation" (Colossians 1:15).

Jesus made many shocking statements to verify His mission. The statements aren't so shocking to us, but they were to the Jewish religious leaders. They viewed God as dwelling in unapproachable light and as someone with whom no one could have a personal relationship. Then

Yeshua descended! He came down to our level so He could bring us up to His. He was the first to encourage us to refer to God as "Father." Too big a stretch of the imagination for the Pharisees, Sadducees, and other religious elite—but Jesus descended not only to tell us but also to show us.

When Philip asked Jesus to show them the Father, He answered by saying, "Have I been with you so long, and yet you have not known Me, Philip? He who has seen Me has seen the Father; so how can you say, 'Show us the Father'?" (John 14:9). Sometimes the forest is right there in front of us, but we can't see it for all those sneaky trees.

Let's not be hard on Philip. At least he was unafraid to ask a question. If he hadn't asked, we wouldn't have that eye-opening answer from Jesus. The Lord is ready to reveal mysteries to us if we are willing to admit our ignorance and ask the question—somewhat like prayer in that God already knows what we need. He already knows what we are thinking and the questions that plague us, but He is waiting for us to put our faith in Him by asking. Ask, seek, knock. God is serious about that.

It should also show us that God is not afraid of our doubts, fears, and questions. Surely He knows what a difficult time we earthlings have when trying to cope with heavenly truth. Perhaps that is why He encourages us to keep being filled with the Spirit (Ephesians 5:18). It is, after all, "the Holy Spirit, whom the Father will send in My name, He will teach you all things, and bring to your remembrance all things that I said to you" (John 14:26).

Some believers have likely been taught that we are not to question God. He never makes any mistakes, you know, so we shouldn't ask questions. True—He does not make mistakes. However, He has given us a lot of mysteries in this life. These mysteries might be for the purpose of getting us to talk to Him in a frank and earnest way. If we hide our feelings of doubt and fear, the Holy Spirit will not be able to calm them.

The word *confess* means "to agree with" or "to acknowledge." If we confess with our mouths the Lord Jesus Christ, we are agreeing with God that He is Lord. If we confess with our mouths that there are some things we don't understand, we are agreeing with God that we are not know-it-alls. And most of us know that everybody else falls into that category—they *don't* know it all.

One thing that can never be said about Jesus is that He beat around the bush. He was plainspoken. And another thing He said plainly that infuriated the religious leaders was that He and the Father were one (John 10:30). To the spiritual man this is proof that Jesus descended from heaven. To the earthly man it appears to be proof that Jesus was insane, demon possessed, or an imposter. The choice is always up to each individual. Jesus is either liar, lunatic, or Lord. He will be loved or hated, but He will not be ignored.

His claim was simple and straightforward. He said it, and it is up to us to deal with it. The Jewish religious leaders dealt with it. They murdered Him. If you want to be your own god, you first must do away with the real one. The "God is dead" movement of yesteryear was an attempt to do just that. It didn't work. He kept showing up in the most unlikely places at the most inconvenient times. He continues showing up in the lives of addicts and alcoholics, in the lives of pimps and prostitutes, in broken homes and broken hearts, in fallen heroes and failed hopes. He just keeps making people new creatures in Christ! He came to make all things new.

And yet society in general continues its attempts to kill God. If one can just get God out of the way, there are no moral absolutes and every person can do what is right in his or her own eyes. Sounds familiar, doesn't it? But God isn't dead and He keeps referring us to those pesky Ten Commandments and that Sermon on the Mount stuff. How intolerant!

The truth that Jesus spoke that pushed the religious elite over the edge was probably this: "Most assuredly, I say to you, before Abraham was, I AM" (John 8:58). To their ears and in their hearts this was the epitome of blasphemy. Jesus was saying that He was with the Father in heaven before He descended to earth. Unthinkable.

How can a mere man be in heaven? And saying, "I AM" makes Him equal with Yahweh.

It was enough to make their heads spin.

Since we aren't going to be too hard on Philip, let's not be too hard on the Pharisees either. Some of them had decades of ingrained teaching that was being challenged by an unemployed carpenter from Galilee. A "nobody" was telling them that God was approachable and that He wants a family to love and bless. He was telling them that Yahweh is opening the Holy of Holies and that common people are welcome to come in— even Gentiles. And He was telling them that He knows this to be true because He is God! Those are a lot of pills to swallow without much water. This doesn't make their crime less serious, but it does make it more explainable or, at least, understandable. Let him who is without sin cast the first stone.

Another side of the name *Jared* is what Paul describes in Ephesians 4:9—"Now this, 'He ascended'—what does it mean but that He also first descended into the lower parts of the earth?" This is likely referring to Jesus's burial. His body was laid in a borrowed tomb. Nevertheless, it is still a descent, as the name *Jared* implies.

Jesus's body descended into the grave. Once again, He has experienced what every human being experiences. He has faced the grim reaper. He knows the sorrow of being separated from family and friends. He knew from the beginning how His life would end. He knew how much pain His mother would feel. What a horrible three days those must have been for Mary!

His descent into the grave, however, was necessary for humanity and for Mary also. Jesus was her son, but she also needed Him as her Savior. And on the third day it is noteworthy that Mary was one of the first to see the empty grave. Later she saw that her son's descent gave way to His ascent. Up from the grave He arose! And as He told the disciples, so Jesus tells all His followers, "Because I live, you will live also" (John 14:19).

Peter adds another descent when he says, "He went and preached to the spirits in prison" (1 Peter 3:19). If heaven is up, the prison that Peter speaks of must be down. Jesus descended to preach. For many this is one of the greatest mysteries in the Holy Bible. What does it mean that Jesus went to the spirits in prison? Why did He go? Were they able to be saved? The answer is beyond the scope of this book. Suffice it to say that He descended to those spirits and He did so for a purpose. This might be a good subject for someone else to write about.

For our study the name *Jared* means "descent." It fits the life of Christ because He descended in several ways. Each of His descents was part of the Father's plan to reach fallen humanity. We fell. Jesus knelt down, descended, to pick us up. Can someone say, "Thank You"?

9

ENOCH:

Man of Preseverance

In part of Isaiah's prophecy of the coming Messiah, he pre-quotes Him as saying, "I have set My face like a flint, and I know that I will not be ashamed" (50:7). This prophecy is fulfilled in Matthew 16:21 when Jesus tells the disciples, "[I] must go to Jerusalem, and suffer many things from the elders and chief priests and scribes, and be killed, and be raised the third day."

These two verses describe the determination of Jesus to do the will of His Father. As has already been said, it was the passion of the Christ to live in obedience to Yahweh. His driving motivation was to fulfill His Father's good pleasure. And it was the Father's will to save humanity through the death and resurrection of His Son.

Thus we come to the name *Enoch,* which means "dedicated; loyal, faithful, or true." This certainly describes Yeshua in His relationship to the Father. Whereas the first Adam was loyal to himself, the last Adam was loyal to God. So dedicated was Jesus to the Father that He would rather die than disobey. It gets even more personal if we will hear Him saying, "I would rather die than live without you!" If He had not died, He would indeed be separated from the human family. We would have no hope. But He did just that—He died. The first Adam tried to gain his life but lost it. The last Adam gave up His life but gained it. Didn't Jesus preach about that? Not only did He preach it—He practiced it as well.

In a society where loyalty is not highly valued anymore, Jesus gives us an opportunity to see loyalty in action. He even prayed in the garden of Gethsemane that if possible His mission be aborted (Luke 22:42). If there were no other way to redeem humanity, then so be it. His only thought was to carry out God's plan for His life.

This was a great example for us to follow but an incredibly difficult one. Not that it was easy for Jesus— not only was He facing death, but He was also facing a particularly painful and humiliating death. His faithfulness earned Him a great reward. His name is above all names. There is no other name whereby we can be saved. He is seated at the right hand of the Father—all because He persevered. He was dedicated, loyal, to the Father's will.

But His obedience also gained humanity great rewards—another understatement. Because of His loyalty, we now have the privilege of becoming the children of God (John 1:12). We are "more than conquerors through Him who loved us" (Romans 8:37). We are given authority to trample on serpents and scorpions and have all power over the enemy (Luke 10:19). The rights and privileges of a child of the King are many and far-reaching.

Due solely to the loyalty of Christ, we have the greatest reward of all. We will spend forever ruling and reigning over all that Jesus has inherited! That's pretty amazing. What did we do to deserve that? Nothing. Yeshua did it. He was faithful unto death. And when He died, we all died (2 Corinthians 5:14). The penalty for sin was paid. "There is therefore now no condemnation to those who are in Christ Jesus, who do not walk according to the flesh, but according to the Spirit" (Romans 8:1).

With that thought in mind, it might be a good time to use a favorite byword: *Wow!* He was loyal to the Father and we got rewarded. Where is the justice in that? It isn't fair. No, it's grace, undeserved favor, unfair blessing—something that God apparently loves to do. Because the Son found favor, all who are redeemed by His blood find favor. Why would anyone turn down so great a gift?

When preaching the Messiah in the book of Acts, Peter says that God has exalted Jesus "to His right hand to be Prince and Savior, to give repentance to Israel and forgiveness of sins (5:31). A man once said that he always wanted to be a generous and giving person because he never got over being saved. This should be the prayer of all of God's children: *Help me to never get over being saved.* May we never take the gift of salvation for granted. In the face of our disloyalty, Messiah remained true. We are all the richer for it.

A conversation recorded by Matthew makes this truth even more amazing—if that's possible. When Jesus was transfigured on the mountain, the Father spoke of Him saying, "This is My beloved Son, in whom I am well pleased. Hear Him!" (17:5). Only one person has ever consistently pleased God. That is His Son. God has said nice things about numerous people. He said that David was a man after His own heart (Acts 13:22). He spoke of

Job as a blameless and upright man (Job 1:8). Abraham was called "the friend of God" (James 2:23). Only one, however, has been called "My beloved Son."

Yahweh said of His Son, "I am well pleased" with Him. Why? He delighted to do the will of God. It was His passion. So if only one person ever consistently pleased God, why are the rest of us so blessed? Part of the answer lies in the story of Cain and Abel. Just before Cain murdered his brother, he was angry that Abel's offering had been accepted while his had not. God came to him and said, "Why are you angry? And why has your countenance fallen? If you do well, will you not be accepted? And if you do not do well, sin lies at the door. And its desire is for you, but you should rule over it" (Genesis 4:6–7).

To "do well" is something every believer can accomplish. Doing well is being loyal to God. Yes, it may cost some persecution. It cost Jesus His life. In some countries, even today, it may cost your life too. For those in America, however, persecution will be a lot less drastic. We may be mocked, laughed at, or scorned. Other believers may even doubt our sincerity when God calls us to do some "strange" things. But all He wants us to do is trust Him. After all, obedience is better than sacrifice.

And obedience is the way of saying to God, "I believe You." Much can be accomplished if believers will do one simple thing: *believe!*

There were times in Jesus's ministry when He could not do many mighty works in certain places. Once, in Matthew 13, Jesus had finished a great discourse beside the sea. He left there and returned to His own country to teach in the synagogue. The listeners were offended at Him and said in essence that He was a nobody. How could a nobody teach such deep truths? We are told that Jesus couldn't do much for them all because of their refusal to believe.

Mark tells the same story in chapter 6. He adds that Jesus marveled at their unbelief. The word *marveled* means "wondered." Even the Son of God couldn't believe that they wouldn't believe! Jesus had the same power, the same ability, the same desire to help them as He had in places where great miracles were done. What hindered Him? Unbelief. As has already been stated, not to believe God is to call Him a liar—a most serious accusation.

We don't read it in Scripture, but Mary was likely persecuted when she told her family and friends that she was with child by the Holy Spirit. Can you imagine the responses? They likely included everything from lighthearted scoffing to accusations of blasphemy. She was even about to have some "confetti" rained down on her—the kind they used in Bible times on people who were accused of crimes against God. Mary also lost her life in obedience to God but gained it again. Her loyalty in the face of persecution has gotten her a place in the Father's hall of fame. Mary is right up there with Sarah, Deborah, and Jephthah's daughter. She will be forever remembered as the one who said to God, "Behold the maidservant of the Lord! Let it be to me according to your word" (Luke 1:38). Talk about dedication! Mary was an instrument in the hands of the master conductor.

For further proof that all believers can be in total submission to the will of God, we must look no further than Joseph in the book of Genesis. His life is perhaps more of an illustration of Christ's life than any other one person in the Holy Bible. Joseph was horribly mistreated by his own brothers but was dedicated to God through all the abuse.

No one knows what went through the mind of Joseph as he spent those years as a stranger in a strange land. Did he ever doubt God's goodness? Did he ever fear that he would never see any of his family again? Was there ever a thought of vengeance? No one knows. A good guess would be "probably." While we are trapped in this world of fantasy, a lot of life's struggles appear hopeless. It's in those times that we are called to be faithful, dedicated. Continuously trusting God to make a way where there is no way is the key to living a victorious life.

This key, however, is not always easy. In all probability, it's never easy. No one ever said it was. Remembering that God is all powerful and that nothing is impossible for Him likely did a lot in seeing Joseph through his difficulties. It can see you through too. When life is closing in on you, that "remembering" thing is sometimes forgotten. We would do good to remember God's love and strength in the good times so we can trust Him in the bad times. Running to Him only in difficult times is somewhat like asking a stranger for a favor.

In the *real* world, where the believer is to dwell, there are no bad times. And God doesn't have any problems. He tells us in Romans 8:28, the verse we love to quote (but seldom practice), that all things can be turned to good things if we trust. Paul instructs, "In everything give thanks; for this is the will of God in Christ Jesus for you (1 Thessalonians 5:18). There's that "will of God" thing again. It's His desire for us to be thankful regardless of the conditions in which we find ourselves.

Be thankful that you are not alone. Joseph may have felt alone at times, but He wasn't. We may feel alone, but we are not. Like Paul, we must learn to be content in whatever state we find ourselves—even in the state of confusion. And there are times when our circumstances are confusing.

A man was asked how he was doing and responded that he was "fine under the circumstances." His friend then asked, "What are you doing *under* the circumstances?" Good question. Don't be *under* your circumstances—get *on top of* them.

When we trust God in all our difficulties, we are being an Enoch. Jesus was an Enoch. Into the Father's hands He commended His Spirit. When we give our problems to God, He solves them by saying, "I don't have any problems. I am the problem-solver." It would be good for all us to stop telling God how big our problems are and to start telling our problems how big our God is. Then problems will become adventures.

Like Enoch, the loyal one, we must reach that place in our relationship with God where He can say, "We're a little closer to my house than we are yours—why don't you just come on home with me?"

10

METHUSELAH:

Man of War

*M*ethuseleh comes from two Hebrew words: *math,* which means "adult," and *shehlakh,* which means "weapon of attack." Put the two together and we have "man who wields an offensive weapon." This implies a person who is attacking an enemy rather than being on the defensive against an enemy who is attacking him. There's a big difference between the two.

This is a great revelation about the heart of God and the mission of Christ. Our God is a warrior! He is on the warpath against an enemy who is attempting to destroy His children. It is sin that separates us from God, and He is determined to remove that barrier—not by a defensive battle but by a full, all-out offensive attack.

Think about it like this: If a bully is not strong enough or brave enough to attack you directly, what is he or she likely to do in an attempt to get at you? The bully might try to harass your children. In Revelation 12 John sees a vision of a woman who gives birth to a male child. A great dragon attempts to eat the child but is thwarted. When he sees that the child has been spared, he determines "to make war with the rest of her offspring, who keep the commandments of God and have the testimony of Jesus Christ" (Revelation 12:17).

This is a vivid illustration of the war that goes on between God and the devil. It began in the garden with an attack against God's first children. It continues to this day with the same attack. God's war is against sin and the enemy, who wants to subject humanity to the consequences of that sin. The consequences, of course, are death—eternal death. Our warrior God is fighting for us against the penalty of sin. Sometimes a person might ask how a loving God can send a soul to hell. The truth is that humanity is already on the way there. God is doing His all to keep us out of hell.

The devil knows that he cannot defeat God. After all, he has tried on several occasions and lost miserably each time. He was thrown out of heaven when he tried to overthrow the true King. He was defeated at the birth of Jesus when he tried to use King Herod to have the child murdered. He was trounced at the cross when he attempted to keep Jesus from fulfilling the Father's mission. And he will be forever defeated when God sends an angel, one angel, to cast him into the pit (Revelation 20:1–3).

Isaiah said of this enemy, "Is this the man who made the earth tremble, who shook kingdoms, who made the world as a wilderness and destroyed its cities, who did not open the house of his prisoners?" (Isaiah 14:16–17). What were we thinking? Why were we afraid of him? We run from the devil and give him credit for defeating us. All the while, God is fighting for us. He is letting the devil run amok so He can show himself mighty to save, heal, and deliver. What better way to train believers to be warriors than to use live ammunition?

There is also an indirect teaching in Methuselah's name that should put us in mind of the armor of God. The first thing is what we have all heard: There is no armor for our back. God does not intend that we retreat—ever. We are children of the King. The King does not retreat—

ever. Neither should His warrior children. Every time the enemy comes against us, it is an opportunity for God to win again. But we must believe that He is able and has our best interests in His heart. If we see every trial as either being sent from God or allowed by God, that perspective will bring the victory much more quickly. We will be less likely to turn and run when we are being trained to turn and fight. The next time your enemy comes against you, pray for God to be glorified in your need.

The enemy is vicious, cruel, and hateful. There is no tactic that he will not use against a child of the king. The King in you is greater than the one who comes against you. Don't just stand your ground—advance. Challenge him. David did just that when he faced Goliath. The recorder of this battle says, "When the Philistine arose and came and drew near to meet David . . . David hurried and ran toward the army to meet the Philistine" (1 Samuel 17:48). David wasn't coming to Goliath as the Welcome Wagon. He wasn't coming to give him a warm hug and friendly handshake. He wasn't coming to present his terms of surrender. David was coming with one purpose in mind: he meant to defeat an enemy who was mocking the God of all glory.

And David hurried and ran toward Goliath. No sight of David's back for the giant! David was moving forward. He was on the offensive. Take the battle to the enemy; don't let him bring it to you. When you wake up in the morning may you hear Satan saying, "Oh, no—he's awake again. Run. Every demon for himself!"

Not only did Goliath not see David's back, but he also probably didn't see that stone coming at his forehead. Too bad for him. He felt it, though. The last thing he remembered was the "thud" of something being buried in his head. May the King's kids be as bold when our enemy scoffs at the true and living God.

Another point to ponder is the phrase "armor of God." At first reading we might see that phrase as meaning the armor that God provides to enable us to quench the fiery arrows of the enemy. We would be correct. However, as with many other facets of God's Word, there is often a deeper meaning. This is true in the case of the armor.

When you read this in Ephesians 6, hear Paul saying, "Put on the whole armor *of God.*" Our armor, then, is God himself! It goes back to the Holy Spirit walking with us and dwelling in us. He covers us inside and out. God told Abraham that He was his shield and his exceedingly great reward. You know that armor that protects you from the enemy's bullets and bombs? "It's me!" says the Lord. "I am your protection. Put me on each day." Without God the battle is lost before it gets started.

David said in Psalm 18:32, "It is God who arms me with strength." Christ in us is not only the hope of glory—He is the only hope for victory over sin and Satan. Yeshua is

our peace not only in the hereafter—He is our power and protection in the here and now.

When Joshua was leading the children of Israel through the promised land and ridding the land of the former inhabitants, God said to him, "You must not fear [your enemies], for the Lord your God Himself fights for you" (Deuteronomy 3:22). Back to David fighting against Goliath, he said, "The Lord does not save with sword and spear; for the battle is the Lord's, and He will give you [Goliath and all the Philistine army] into our hands" (1 Samuel 17:47).

David's words were a prophecy of the weapon that God would use to defeat sin and the enemy who wants to bind us in it. His weapon, of course, is the Christ. God's only begotten Son is the one who fights for us and gives our enemy into our hands.

There may be some believers who have the idea that they must fight these battles in their own strength and with their own resources. If this is not true even in the world of human armies, why would it be true in the real, everyday world? An army of human soldiers is trained and equipped by those for whom they are fighting. Their country provides their needs. In the case of Christian soldiers, we are trained and equipped by our heavenly Father through His Holy Spirit. He teaches our hands to war and our fingers to battle (Psalm 144:1). Then He equips us with the weapon with which to fight, the indwelling Holy Spirit.

There are a few instances in the Word in which God won a decisive victory without having anyone raise a sword or shoot an arrow. Once He did it by sending the choir to lead the battle! That's right, the choir (2 Chronicles 20).

He took down the walls of Jericho not with an army or a choir but with a shout of praise and the blowing of trumpets (Joshua 6).

One time in the life of Elisha God struck the opposing army with blindness. They couldn't even see who or where their enemy was (2 Kings 6).

Our warrior God has many weapons He uses to fight for His people. He gives us physical examples in the Old Testament to teach us that His weapons are limitless. Once He used hailstones (Joshua 10), another time He said He would use hornets (Exodus 23), and for another battle He used fear (Judges 7).

Our God has never lost a battle and He will not lose the war against sin. Those examples from the Old Testament are shown so we can apply their outcome to our battles against the devil. All of God's children are mighty men of valor when we realize that our weapon is the Lord Jesus Christ. He reveals himself in different ways in the battles, but it is always Jesus who is the primary weapon.

The battles and wars of the Old Testament give us encouragement to believe that God will win the battles now just as He did then. Has God ever used a doctor or medicine to heal or cure a disease? Has He ever sent an angel to minister in a time of distress? Did someone ever speak a word of faith or encouragement to you at just the right moment? Have you ever received a financial blessing just in the nick of time? Hmm—who do you suppose was behind all those "coincidences"? Maybe God was showing off the cache of weapons He has to work with through His Son.

Sometimes believers are like the little boy who was playing on the roof and began sliding toward the edge and couldn't stop. In just a few feet he would be going over and would plummet to the ground. He cried out, "Oh, God, help me!" Just at that moment his pants caught on a nail stopping his descent. When he realized he had been spared a sure fall, he said, "Never mind, God—a nail caught my pants!"

Are we guilty of the same? We praise the doctor or the medicine when we would have neither if God did not provide intelligence and ability for both. Yes, we should thank the doctor or the one who spoke the word of faith or the one who sent the financial blessing, but the source of each and every blessing is Yeshua! He is the Father's weapon of choice—not only to fight the ravages of sin but also to fight those everyday battles of life that are an attempt to get us to deny the power of God.

Notice, too, that Methuselah lived longer than any of the other patriarchs. Could this be an allusion to the endlessness of Christ's victory? Just something to think about. We do know, however, that the life of Jesus will never end, so why would we think His power to save and deliver will end?

11

LAMECH:
Man of Power

Leh'-mek means "powerful." Looking at it from another point of view, it means "full of power." Whatever is full of power has no place in its being for that which does not have power. *Full* means, well, "full"—no empty place, no grey areas. Every part is filled with the same amount of power. That's why God is referred to as "the Almighty," "the All-Powerful." There is no part of God that is not filled with power. He is the power of salvation, healing, and deliverance. He asked Sarah, "Is anything too hard for the Lord?" (Genesis 18:14). A parted sea, a rock gushing with water, bread from heaven, a baby born from a ninety-year-old woman and a hundred-year-old man—impossible? Not for the God of all power!

The miracles mentioned above are from the Old Testament. They and others were performed by God after He had instructed someone (Moses, Joshua, Abraham, and others) to call on Him. This limitless power of God, however, confronts humanity face to face in the life of Christ. He is not a vessel that God uses to call on so He can do something supernatural. Jesus is the supernatural. He is the power of God revealed in the flesh. You know, if you want something done right . . .

The ultimate revelation of the overpowering power of God in Christ is most certainly the resurrection. The resurrection was the overthrowing and total defeat of our last and greatest enemy. When Jesus took on death He looked it straight in the eye—and death backed down! Jesus was "declared to be the Son of God *with power* according to the Spirit of holiness, by the resurrection from the dead" (Romans 1:4, emphasis added).

Yes, there was great power in all the miracles, signs, and wonders performed by Jesus. Restoring sight to the blind is no magician's trick. Causing crippled legs to walk can't be done by sleight of hand. Changing water to wine isn't accomplished with smoke and mirrors. These were simply the appetizers, if you will. They preceded the greatest banquet of God's power ever seen. That power was witnessed and verified when Jesus was raised from the dead.

Part of Jesus's ministry was to give some pre-resurrection examples of what the Father was going to do in His life. He raised a twelve-year-old girl back to life. He stopped a funeral procession to give life back to a widow's only son. The most well-known miracle of resurrection was when Jesus raised His friend Lazarus from the dead. Each of these people, however, died again. Each of them had to experience breathing his or her last breath a second time. However, Christ's resurrection was so powerful that He will never die again. And because He will never die again, neither will those who have been born again.

God's math is unique. In the case of resurrection it goes like this: If you are born once, you will die twice; if you are born twice, you will die once. Of course, the instances of Lazarus, Jairus's daughter, and the widow's son are exceptions to the rule. They were given as examples of the life-giving, death-defeating power of God before the ultimate example was revealed. It's good that God causes the sun to rise gradually rather than suddenly bursting into the sky each morning. The resurrections just cited are gentle sunrises. They prepared the people for the irreversible resurrection. Isn't God the best you've ever seen? The best what? The best *everything.* He does all things for His glory and for our blessing—all things. Yes, even that.

Prior to raising Lazarus, Jesus asked Mary and Martha if they believed their brother would live again. They both answered that they did believe—that he would live again at the resurrection of the last day. Jesus said, "I am the resurrection and the life" (John 11:25). Here's that byword again: *Wow!* Jesus does not simply *have* life—He *is* life. He is the reason we exist. He is the source of our existence. He is the spring that gives water to the stream, the pond, the lake, the river.

The Christ, the anointed one, is the sight that opens blind eyes. He is the strength that animates crippled legs. He is the compassion that heals broken hearts, the hope that restores faded dreams, the voice that calls a dead spirit to live again. As a great writer once wrote, "No wonder they call Him the Savior" (Max Lucado, *No Wonder They Call Him the Savior* [Nashville: Thomas Nelson Publishing, 1986]).

Jesus told His disciples—and us—"I am the way, the truth, and the life" (John 14:6). He wasn't just stating that He knew how to get somewhere or that He understood the difference between fact and fiction or that He merely existed. His words invite us to enter into Him and experience who He is. He is the yellow brick road, the best policy, the air that we breathe. All things come from Him and exist in Him (Revelation 4:11). That's a mighty big God—big enough to carry the sins of the world, big enough to take those sins to Hades and come back without them (Acts 2:30–32).

Neither did His power end when He left the earth. He gave us His Holy Spirit to be our comforter, teacher, and helper. The third person of the Trinity, the Holy Spirit, is God's power on earth. In Acts 1:8 Jesus said, "You shall receive power when the Holy Spirit has come upon you." This promise and power are not for those first disciples only. They are for all disciples in every age (John 17:20–21).

Many believers have been taught that the word *power* in Acts 1:8 is the word *doo'-nam-is* and is where we get the English word *dynamite*. True—and yet so much more. It literally means a "miraculous force." Since miracles are from the real world, the supernatural one, it wouldn't be a stretch of the imagination to say that they are explosive. They explode into our little fantasy world by the power of God, the Holy Spirit. And like the explosion of dynamite, miracles sometimes startle us—even when we expect them. (May we be startled more often.)

For the Holy Spirit, however, miracles are just God being God. Miracles are what He does, where He lives, and who He is. Miracles are the bricks of which the kingdom of God are made. Is that why Jesus taught us to pray, "Thy kingdom come"? Is that perhaps a reason that we, the body of Christ, do not see more power in our lives today?

Paul warned us that the last days before the return of Christ would be perilous. When he wrote to Timothy he said that part of the reason for the difficulties would be the fault of the church. In 2 Timothy 3:5 he said there would be "a form of godliness but denying its power." Yes, the word for *power* there is *doo'-nam-is*. We expect no power from the world systems, so Paul must be speaking of the church. In the last days there will be little or no power in the church. Someone once said that if the Holy Spirit left most churches in America, neither the pulpit nor the people would know it. They would continue on in their rituals and routines.

Since the ultimate power of God is the resurrection, what does denying the power mean to us? Resurrection means going from death to life. God is not so interested in making bad people into good people. However, He *is* passionate about making dead people live. When one is born again, he or she will likely become a good person. We rarely if ever see a born-again Christian turn to cocaine after he or she is saved. We do see a lot of cocaine-users stop using the drug and clean up their lives after being saved. Seems that people who are alive by the power of God want to be good. Mostly we see sinners turn away from sin when they are redeemed. They don't turn back to sin. So bad people will likely become good people after they are saved, but they must first become alive people.

The passion of God is to make each person a new creature in Christ by bringing him or her back from the dead. We as believers are told that before our transformation we were dead in our trespasses and sins (Ephesians 2:1). We were alive once (Romans 7:9), but we died. God now wants to resurrect us through faith in the

Lord Jesus Christ and the power of His Holy Spirit. In the last days there will be a denial of that power. It will be said that we must simply think positive and turn over a new leaf. There's nothing wrong with thinking positive—Paul instructs us to do just that in Philippians 4:8.

The power of positive thinking, however, can spiral downward into a denial of God's power to change our lives. In such cases the church becomes a social club. We attend meetings and pay our dues. Some have said that the church becomes a museum for saints rather than a hospital for sinners. Positive thinking can carry you a good way down the road, but a new heart will carry you all the way home.

A resurrected life is the supreme demonstration of the power of God. There are other ways, however, that God makes His power known. The world and the church need to see transformed lives. The best advertisement God has is a life that had been severely damaged by sin but has been brought to life by God's wonder-working power. Both the world and the church need to see the power of God in the daily life of the believer.

Too often we believers encounter troubles in our lives and don't even think about asking God to glorify himself in those troubles. We are so very quick to take our problems to the doctor, the lawyer, the counselor, the banker, the psychiatrist, and so on. There is no sin in seeking human help—the sin is in not seeking God first. Remember what Jesus said: "Seek first the kingdom of God and His righteousness, and all these things shall be added to you" (Matthew 6:33).

Jesus was speaking directly about food and clothing in that verse, but the principal thing is to keep God first. Ask Him first. The main thing is to keep the main thing the main thing. God is the main thing. If you sever an artery while using the skill saw, it might seem a waste of time to ask God if He wants you to go to the emergency room. In the case of severed arteries or severed anythings, perhaps you can pray for Him to be glorified in the injury while you are on the way to the hospital. He might just give you grace to make it. Keep this in mind too: unbelievers have problems, whereas believers have *adventures*. That severed artery could be just another adventure!

Earlier it was said that God does the impossible as simply as some people can fall off a log. There is nothing impossible for God. He is all-powerful. This is why a believer has adventures. The Father has no problems—why should His children? The Father has only solutions and cures. In fact, He *is* the solution and the cure. That's why we need to ask Him first. He knows the answer before there's a question. When we factor God into the equation, life becomes one big adventure.

Moses always got the answer by telling God that He had a problem: "We're between the devil and the deep blue sea. We have no water, no food, and too much time on our hands. God, you have a problem." By His actions that followed, God was responding by saying, "I don't have problems. What is that in your hand?" Moses learned that the power of God was the evidence that life is an adventure. "What will God do next? How will my Father fix this fiasco? Well, here's another fine mess I've gotten myself into. From which direction will God come this time?" Look to God first. He's there before we even realize He's on the way.

David had a situation in his life (understatement alert) that easily could have turned into disaster if he had not looked to his shepherd (God) first. In 1 Samuel 30 David and his mighty men of valor have been on a shopping spree. When they return to Ziklag, their home base, they find the city burned and all their possessions stolen. Even their wives and children have been taken.

Some people would have immediately pursued the invaders. David had the ephod brought to him so he could ask God what His plan was. David said, "Shall I pursue this troop? Shall I overtake them?" (1 Samuel 30:7). God answered him, "Pursue, for you shall surely overtake them and without fail recover all" (v. 8). The power of God prevails again.

When the adventure seems a bit intense, don't forget who has the power to keep you on the right road. Remember who is the cure for every disease, the tamer of every lion, the retardant of every fire, the slayer of every giant. *Lamech* means "powerful." His name speaks of the Christ, who is full of power—all power, no weakness.

12

NOAH:
Man of Rest

How great is our God! *Noah*—what a perfect way to end the names of the men who represent the life and saving graces of the Christ! *No'-akh* is the only name whose meaning is given to us. In Genesis 5:29 Lamech says, "This one will comfort us concerning our work and the toil of our hands, because of the ground which the Lord has cursed."

Lamech's prophecy was true, but he probably did not realize that his son's name and ministry went much deeper than the work and toil of our hands. The name *Noah* means "rest." Lamech said that Noah will comfort us. The word *comfort* means "sigh or breathe." We have heard that something long awaited was like a breath of fresh air. The rest that is spoken of in the name *Noah* is that breath of fresh air. He is a brand-new start for humanity.

Before Adam's rebellion God had already named the patriarchs. Each one reflected an aspect of Christ. He ends with Noah, our rest, who is going to obey the Lord and give humanity a fresh start. The earth will die and live again. The animals will die and live again. Humanity will die and live again—all through the power of God and the faithfulness of Noah, the man who found grace in the eyes of the Lord.

Obviously this is prophecy, a foretelling of the future. God must have given Lamech a glimpse of what He was going to do through the life of Noah. If Lamech had seen further into the future, he would have observed the Son of God doing the same thing.

"Come to Me . . . and I will give you rest" (Matthew 11:28), says the Master—not rest from the work of our hands but rest from the work of self-righteousness, the work of self-sufficiency, the work of trying to please God by being good. Whew! A breath of fresh air, a sigh of thanksgiving. Now the work of God is to believe on His Son (John 6:29).

Jesus has freed us from the law of sin and death and delivered us to the law of life and liberty. For centuries salvation was anchored in keeping the law of Moses. People had labored under the belief that the law could save them. Offer the sacrifices, make the pilgrimages, celebrate the feasts, observe the holy days. The problem was that keeping the law became their salvation. If one kept the law, he or she pleased God, and if God was pleased, that person was glory bound. The trouble, however, was that no one could keep the law.

No one was *intended* to keep the law. It couldn't be done. The standard was too high to be reached, too holy to be attained. "The law was our tutor to bring us to Christ, that we might be justified by faith" (Galatians 3:24). When someone realizes that his or her work is futile and is making no progress, that person has a choice. He or she can keep doing the same thing while expecting a different result (we know what word that defines). Or he can try something altogether different.

God already knew from the beginning that He was going to do something different. He had laid down the law as a way of showing us that His plan all along was going to be different--because He is different, He is holy.

It's interesting that *holy* comes to us in several different words, but within each one is the meaning "dedicate." (Remember Enoch?) Something that is dedicated is set apart for a special purpose. Sometimes we are frightened by the word *sanctify* or *sanctification*. The truth is that we are most often frightened by what we do not understand. It isn't that anyone is stupid but that he or she is ignorant. To be sanctified simply means to be set apart for a special or unique purpose.

This is our God! He is one of a kind! He is different from all other gods. In Psalm 86:8 David said it this way: "Among the gods there is none like You, O Lord; nor are there any works like Your works." Our God is unique, different, holy, sanctified. And He wants His children to be like Him. After all, we are created in His image and after His likeness. In fact, He said to us, "You shall be holy to Me, for I the Lord am holy, and have separated you from the peoples, that you should be Mine" (Leviticus 20:26).

We can be different because our God is different. Think of it like this: "You shall be well because I am well; you shall be rich because I am rich; you shall be strong because I am strong." We are all this—and much more— because our Father is the King. We are heirs of all He is and all He has (Romans 8:17). What an incredible gift is this rest that God offers to us! Stop trying and start trusting.

The rest that Christ offers us is what makes Christianity different from all other belief systems. It has been said that Christianity is not a religion—it's a relationship. Bingo! Believers are not better than people who have other beliefs, but we are certainly better off. The other beliefs (you can name them) are an attempt to please a deity in an attempt to find enough favor with said deity in an attempt to gain an eternal reward from the aforementioned deity. Got it?

Our God is different. He did something different. He tells us to enter into His rest. What? We must work for everything, right? Not salvation. Jesus paid it all. He said, "It is finished!" (John 19:30). There is nothing that can be added to what He has done. Salvation isn't *Jesus and* or *Jesus plus* or *Jesus along with*. Salvation is *Jesus*—period!

The writer of Hebrews said it this way: "God, who at various times and in various ways spoke in time past to the fathers by the prophets, has in these last days spoken to us by His Son" (1:1–2). You might say that Jesus is the Father's final answer. Actually He was His first answer too, but it took some time to get the world ready to hear the message. So God sent prophets, priests, and kings to prepare the way. Some of the very people who should have been first to recognize the different message of rest either didn't get it or didn't want it. Was that two thousand years ago? Sounds a lot like now.

The work that God wants us to do, then, is to rest— rest in Him, rest in what He has done for us through Christ. After all, a friend of the Son's is a friend of the Father's. When someone asks why you should be allowed in heaven, tell the person that Jesus invited you to come and that you accepted the invitation. There was no contest to win, no luck of the draw, no rite of passage, no price to pay. He said, "Follow Me." If you follow, you make a brilliant choice. If you throw away the invitation, forget about it, or get too busy to respond, you miss the greatest celebration ever planned. God calls it a "marriage supper" (Revelation 19:9).

Being saved by the grace of God through faith in the blood of Christ is God's rest for us, rest from trying to please God. Only one person ever totally pleased God. When you receive His forgiveness and turn away from your sins to follow Jesus, God accepts you into His beloved. And again, God is always pleased with His beloved. Anyone who is a new creature in Christ is resting comfortably in God's amazing grace.

The rest we find in Christ does not end with salvation. It is simply the beginning of a journey to a new home, a final rest, a rest without sickness, sorrow, sin, or Satan. While resting in Christ in the here and now we still must deal with trials and temptations. When we reach that final rest, however, "our light affliction, which is but for a moment" (2 Corinthians 4:17), will be as if it had never happened. Such is the eternal rest to which our Savior invites us.

How blessed are we to enter such rest? Jesus told a parable in Matthew 22 about a king who prepared a banquet for his son's wedding (sounds familiar already). He invited many guests. The invited ones, however, laughed at the king and went about their business. Some even beat the servants who brought the king's invitation to them. The king then invited guests from the highways to attend the celebration.

A strange thing happens as the party is getting started. The king sees a man in the crowd who is not wearing a wedding garment. He instructs his servants to bind the man hand and foot and cast him out into the darkness. It seems a bit harsh. Was the king taking out his anger at the guests who refused the invitation on a man who wasn't dressed properly?

In Jesus's time honored guests at such an exclusive banquet would wear long white robes to identify them as invited ones. The wearing of the garment said, "I am special. I am here at the king's bidding." The garment identified the guest as a personal friend of the king— quite the status symbol, revealing the respect the king had for the guest. A person who was not wearing such a garment was an intruder, an enemy. This person would therefore be removed from the party as we would want a cancer removed from our bodies.

The parable, therefore, is not about a king who is a cruel tyrant. It is told to teach us the high esteem that the Father has for His Son. It is a commentary on the high price that Jesus paid for us to be able to attend His marriage supper. And it is a revelation of the love, honor, and respect we owe to Jesus. He is our wedding garment. If one expects to gain heaven without putting on Christ, he is in for a rude awakening. When we do put Him on as our robe, He identifies us as a friend of the king.

No one will see the Father unless he or she comes to Him through the Son (John 14:6) and no one will come to the Son unless the Father draws him or her (John 6:44). The love and respect between Yahweh and Yeshua is beyond explanation or definition. It is like Paul ascending to the third heaven and hearing words so holy that he could not repeat them. The love between Father and Son is of such magnitude. We can't fathom it, but we know that God is serious about His love for the Son. He is serious when He says that Jesus is the only way to approach the throne of grace. He is the only way to enter God's rest.

Noah—man of rest. He was prophesied to bring comfort concerning the work of our hands. His name reveals Christ, the one who brings comfort concerning the work of our souls and spirits. Rest in Jesus—He is your every need supplied.

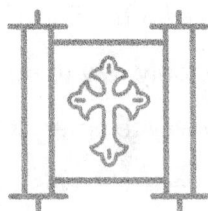

$$\diamondsuit\!\!\diamondsuit$$

CONCLUSION

And so as Solomon said, "Let us hear the conclusion of the whole matter" (Ecclesiastes 12:13). It is just this: our loving and holy God has revealed to us His perfect plan for saving humanity. He began this revelation with a man of earth and ends with a man of rest. God came to us through His Son in a human body, a body of the earth. He came to reconcile the world to himself. That reconciliation cost Him His life, and therefore He was in this world for only a brief time. He took our place and paid the penalty for the sins we had committed. He experienced all the pain and sorrow that we endure. He was the possessor of heaven and earth, yet gave it all up to save humanity. He gave himself as a sacrifice of praise to the Father. He descended into our world to enable us to ascend to His. He stood strong against the temptations to abandon the Father's plan.

He fought valiantly against the enemy in the battle to redeem humanity. His power was displayed in the weakness of the cross. He won! He gave us rest in the here and now *and* in the hereafter.

The story of God's redeeming grace is a magnificent tale of love, sacrifice, commitment, and victory. And it is amazing that He told us about it in the names of twelve men. Thousands of years before the birth of Christ, God revealed to us what He was going to do. It can't be overemphasized: the entire Holy Bible points us to God's gift of eternal life through Jesus Christ. The Old Testament points forward to Jesus; the Gospels reveal Jesus; the remainder of the New Testament points back to Jesus. It's as if there is only one way for a man to escape eternal death! Hmm. And God began telling this astonishing story with the creation of the very first human! He continued His story through the naming of the following eleven descendants of Adam.

It's difficult not to be overwhelmed by the mercies of God when He has gone to such great lengths to make himself known. Any belief system that does not acknowledge Yahweh as the Source behind all creation falls short of knowing and proclaiming the truth. And knowing the truth sets us free to understand the heart of our king. Surely the one who has shown us His Son in the names of these twelve men will never leave us nor forsake us. He took us to raise.

God wants us to know Him. He wants us to have an intimate relationship with Him. He wants us to receive His love and blessings. He is passionate for us to have His kingdom. All that He created was given to us as a gift. Read the Genesis account of creation. God created a beautiful, perfect world. He then gave it to His favorites. When we threw that gift away, He already had another gift at the ready. In the beginning God said, "I have given you a garden—now trust Me to care for you." In these last days He is saying, "Trust Me to care for you and I will give you a garden." Through faith in Christ, we can be as sure of being in that garden as if we were already there—not because of our goodness or worthiness but because that is what God wants to do. You have heard it said that nails did not keep Jesus on the cross—love kept Him there. Truth.

Now "We love Him because He first loved us" (1 John 4:19). There is no pretense or hypocrisy. There is nothing about us that deserves the love of the Father. He loves us because He loves us. No one deserves it, can earn it, or buy it. God has so much love to give—all we can do is accept it and say, "Thank You."

Once again, the mind-boggling truth in this study is that God is so in love with His children that He gives us a glimpse of it in the names He gives to His first dozen children. Hopefully, if nothing else, you have gained an understanding of a way God makes a revelation to us without putting it on a silver platter. There are many names and words in His Word that will open doors for His people to know Him more intimately. Our part is to get at it with pick and shovel. If you don't have those, determination and passion will do.

May the Father bless you richly as you dig more deeply into His love each day. Shalom!